Undefeated, Untied, and Uninvited

A Documentary of the 1951
University of San Francisco Dons Football Team

Undefeated, Untied, and Uninvited

A Documentary of the 1951
University of San Francisco Dons Football Team

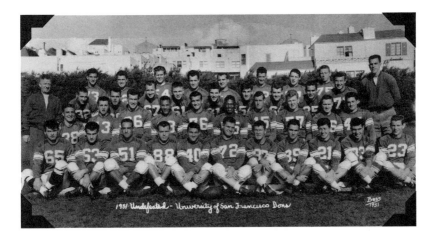

Kristine Setting Clark

Forewords by
Pro Football Hall of Fame Members
Gino Marchetti, Ollie Matson, and Bob St. Clair,
and
National Football League Official
Burl Toler

Director of Operations: Robin L. Howland
Project Manager: Bryan K. Howland
Editor: Word Perfect
Book and Cover Design: m2design group

10 9 8 7 6 5 4 3 2 1
ISBN 1-58000-107-6

Griffin Publishing Group
18022 Cowan, Suite 202
Irvine, California 92614
www.griffinpublishiing.com

Manufactured in the United States of America

"It's not the critic who counts. It's not the man who points out when a strong man stumbles or when the doer of deeds could have done better. It's the man who is actually in the arena; the doer of the deed. The man whose face is marked by sweat, blood and tears. The man who knows, in the end, the triumph of high achievement: the man whose heart will never be among those cold and timid ones who know neither victory nor defeat."

—Theodore Roosevelt
Twenty-sixth President of the United States

This book is dedicated to those doers of the deed

THE 1951 DONS

I would like to especially thank the following people:

To Lorrie Aguirre Laurence: Thank you for your time, your belief and your devotion to this story; and for your guidance and expertise in helping me to write this book. I could not have done it without you.

To Bill Henneberry: Thanks for keeping the faith in me and in my ability to tell this wonderful story to the rest of the world.

To Bob St. Clair: You are an extraordinary person and a wonderful friend. Thank you for all your help, your candidness and your advice. And thank you so very much for always being there for me.

To my uncle, Fred Setting: Without you there would not be any pictures in this book! Thank you for the time and effort you gave in helping to bring this story to life.

To my husband, Bill: You've always supported my dreams and my ambitions and have always been there for me. You are and always will be my best friend, and I love you for that.

And my sincere thanks to the many other people who have helped to make this book possible.

ACKNOWLEDGEMENTS

UNIVERSITY OF SAN FRANCISCO
Fr. Kotlanger
Fr. Lo Schiavo
Don Mc Laughlin
Dick Rafetto
Russ Sabini
USF Archives
USF Yearbook

FRIENDS AND FAMILY
Elizabeth De Long (Mike)
Mark Huynh - Galileo High School
Madeline Kuharich (Joe)
Bill Kuharich
Joan Marchetti (Gino)
Mary Matson (Ollie)
Franklin Mieuli
Robert Schnitzer -
   Galileo High School
Ann St. Clair (Bob)
Lynn St. Clair-Gretton

NATIONAL FOOTBALL LEAGUE
Baltimore (Indianapolis) Colts
Chicago Bears
Dan Colchico
Detroit Lions
Art Donovan
Jimmy Johnson
Billy Kilmer
Don Klosterman
Los Angeles (St. Louis) Rams
Hugh Mc Elhenny
Lenny Moore
National Football League
Leo Nomellini
R. C. Owens
Joe Perry

Pro Football Hall of Fame
San Francisco 49ers
Gordy Soltau
Dick Stanfel
Paul Tagliabue
Y. A. Tittle
Keena Turner
Johnny Unitas
Washington Redskins
Billy Wilson

MEDIA
Dave Anderson - New York Times
Ira Blue - Sportscaster
Kathy Davis - NFL Films
Chris Gargano - Fox Sports
Noah Griffin - Writer and Poet
Joe Horrigan - Pro Football Hall
   of Fame
Kezar Stadium Archives
George Krause - Photographer
Judy Kuntz - Pro Football Hall
   of Fame
Charles Mc Dermid -
   San Francisco Examiner
Bill Plaschke - Los Angeles Times
Grantland Rice - Sportswriter
Steve Sabol - NFL Films
San Francisco Parks and
   Recreation Department

GOVERNMENT OFFICIALS
Senator Barbara Boxer
San Francisco Mayor
   Willie Brown
Senator Dianne Feinstein
Congressman Steve Largent
John Olmsby - Assistant to
   Senator Barbara Boxer
Congresswoman Lynn Woolsey

CONTENTS

INTRODUCTION

At the conclusion of his 2000 Pro Football Hall of Fame enshrinement speech, Howie Long stated, "I still believe that baseball is America's favorite pastime, but football is truly America's passion." To the people of San Francisco who remember, this statement will continue to hold true whenever there's mention of the Hilltop's first, last, and only football champions.

They had the entire City behind them. *Good Night Irene* became their theme song and was sung at every home game while fans stood and white handkerchiefs waved. Steve Sabol of NFL Films referred to them as, "the 'magnificent eleven' that no one had ever heard of." A small college with a big-time lineup; they were the undefeated, the untied, the 1951 University of San Francisco Dons football team.

This is their story. A story of an urban Jesuit university's struggle to find its place in the world of big-time college football only to be stopped short by the ignorance of racial discrimination. It was a season marked by irony: A football team from a Division I basketball school that was ignored by history.

In an era of crew cuts, two-way players, and helmets without face masks, this USF team was one of the best, if not *the best* college football team ever to play the game. They exhibited a roster of players and personnel that read like a who's who of gridiron heroes; but when it came time to announce the schools who would be granted a bowl bid, *teams with "Negro players" would be avoided at all costs.*

Many football fans may be unaware that this '51 team produced nine future NFL players; and that was when the league had only twelve teams. It would have been ten, but one, Burl Toler, who was drafted by the Cleveland Browns in his junior year was so severely injured in the '52 College All Star game that he never played again. He later went on to become the first black official in the NFL; a position bestowed upon him by NFL Commissioner and future Hall of Famer Pete Rozelle, who, coincidentally, was the Don's "athletic news director" in 1951. Of the remaining nine players, five made it to the Pro Bowl and three of those five were inducted into Pro Football's Hall of Fame; the most ever from a single college team. The three inductees were Bob St. Clair, Ollie Matson, and Gino Marchetti. Matson and Marchetti were inducted into the Hall in 1972—their first year of eligibility. They were to become the only college teammates to claim this honor.

Another little-known fact is that the 1950 USF football team (which included the 51 team members) fielded two more NFL draftees bringing the two team total to twelve. Dick Stanfel, a guard on that '50 team, was an All Pro with the Detroit Lions, and a Senior nominee finalist in the 1993 Hall of Fame selection. Roy Barni, a halfback on that same team, was drafted by the Chicago Cardinals.

The 1957 Pro Bowl game reunited teammates Ed Brown (Bears), Gino Marchetti (Colts), Ollie Matson (Cardinals), Bob St. Clair (49ers) and '50 teammate, Dick Stanfel (Lions).

The coach of the team was Joe Kuharich (former Notre Dame All-American and future Chicago Cardinals', Washington Redskins' and Philadelphia Eagles' coach). Following the footsteps of Knute Rockne, Kuharich conditioned his team both physically and mentally to outplay anyone; but more than that he instilled in his players a sense of loyalty and admiration (as well as fear) that would extend far beyond the playing field.

This 1951 gridiron team would be the last of its kind to be fielded by USF and it would be, by far, the one who would leave a lasting imprint on the memory of many in this City by the Bay.

Undefeated, Untied, and Uninvited goes behind the scenes to explore the successes and challenges that faced the Dons. It is a story told from the "inside", in the players' own words, in the words of those closest to them, and through the eyes and ears of the media. Everything in here, from scores to stats to quotes, is as accurate as possible

Return with us now to relive this unforgettable season as Joe Kuharich and his "boys of autumn" discover the true meaning of "autumn fever." The season has begun, and Northern California is astounded by the talent that surrounds the University of San Francisco's varsity football team. The Dons are uniquely gifted, exceptionally physical in size and strength and highly skilled. And, unlike most college teams, they are integrated.....a rarity for 1951.

FOREWORD

GINO MARCHETTI

We are very fortunate people—those of us who have "Lady Luck" on our side. Or should I call her a Good Angel?" One day in 1948 while driving around in my hometown of Antioch, California, Lady Luck whispered in my ear, "Drive down F Street." So I did. There I saw a strange car parked in front of my house. This was the beginning of my career in football. Inside the house were a couple of scouts from Modesto Junior College who were recruiting my younger brother, Angelo. After he agreed to go to Modesto, they turned to me and said, "You're kind of big, too. Why don't you tag along?"

Luck played a big part in my start in football, but hard work kept me there. The kind of hard work and intense training that I had at the University of San Francisco under the coaching of Joe Kuharich.

It was at USF that I learned the discipline needed by every athlete who wants to be a success in his career. It was there that I felt the real fellowship with my teammates that carried over into professional sports. Coach Kuharich was, by his own example, a pillar of strength and inspiration to me and to the San Francisco Dons. Many of the lessons I had learned from Coach Joe brought me success not only throughout my football career, but also in the business world. Lessons on loyalty, honesty, and perseverance were just a few of the character building qualities he taught us.

The University of San Francisco had a tremendous football scouting staff in those years. Brad Lynn was a good example of their recruiting skill. When you have all the pieces in the puzzle, you can create a masterpiece. And look at the team that these people created—the 1951 Dons: a truly great college team of its time! After their college days were over, these men went on to become leaders in their chosen careers, whether it was in the world of sports or in the business sector. I am very proud to have known them and to have been their friend.

Last, but not least, I remember Father Jim Giambastiani, who made sure we attended class and gave us a great deal of spiritual guidance. He was our "Good Shepherd" on earth and has a special place in the hearts of those he taught. Many a time he came to my room to "remind" me that I was due in class.

Whether I call it "luck" or "divine providence," I am very grateful for the experiences life has given to me. We live in a country full of opportunities and, with the right guidance, we can make the best of them.

Thank you, University of San Francisco, for providing the foundation and the building blocks to a successful and contented life. But thank you most of all for the memories!

—Gino Marchetti

Gino Marchetti

OLLIE MATSON

Making a decision back in those days was somewhat easy because not many universities went after Black athletes. After graduating from George Washington High School and City College of San Francisco, I visited a few universities and, with the guidance of my mother, decided that USF was for me. Funny that I never before noticed that little university on the "Hilltop" as it was referred to back then; and to think it was only a few blocks from my home.

When I think of USF, I remember the many memories of my time spent at the University. One memory that will forever remain with me is the USF fans. When it became evident that we had a game wrapped up, our entire rooting section would stand and sing *Good Night Irene, Irene Good Night*. That was the greatest because you knew you had the City behind you; and when you have an entire city behind you, that's it. I really thought we owned San Francisco. I believed that it was our city.

Even though a lot of people didn't realize how good we were until later on, I always felt that we had the finest team in the nation that year. I honestly believe that if we could have kept that '51 team together and entered the NFL as pros, within two to three years we would have been the champions! I really believe that. We were a great team but society was not ready for us in the '50's.

"Too soon for my time" seemed to be the story of my life. You see, I also loved track and field and in 1952 at the Helsinki Olympics, I was awarded a silver medal and a bronze medal. The honor was great but back then no endorsement offers followed. Today I look at these young athletes and think, "If they have talent and work at that talent, the sky's the limit."

Looking back I have very few regrets about my decision to attend USF. We were small enough to have a close relationship among our team members and other classmates, but still good enough to acquire national recognition. Our records could stand up against any university's.

The University of San Francisco was the foundation to my successes in life. It built character and gave me the confidence, as well as the opportunity, to excel throughout my sports and business careers. There is no reason for anyone to try to use racism as an escape. You can be anything you want to be.

I would like to thank USF, the Jesuits, Coach Kuharich and his staff, and my teammates for the education and inspiration that they have given to me that I have so cherished throughout the past 50 years.

—Ollie Matson

Ollie Matson

BOB ST. CLAIR

Who would have ever thought that a hooligan born in San Francisco's Mission District and raised in the city's Ingleside District would be blessed with the athletic ability to rise to the pinnacle of professional football's greatest accolade—The Hall of Fame? And if that weren't enough, to have the very field at Kezar Stadium that he had called home and played upon for 18 seasons, be named Bob St. Clair Field!

Early in life I learned to play sports on the playground at Farragut Elementary School on Ocean Avenue. One day, while playing in a neighborhood pickup game of football, one of the older kids broke my nose. It was at that very moment that I had decided that football wasn't all it was cracked up to be and made the decision to concentrate on a sport somewhat less physically damaging, like baseball or basketball. That idea turned out to be short lived.

Upon entering the tenth grade at Polytechnic High School I decided to give football another try. At 15 years old, I stood 5'10" and weighed in at 160 pounds. Even though I had made the team, I was still somewhat awkward and not exactly what one would regard as "outstanding football material." The following year I had grown to 6'4" and weighed in at 210 pounds.

All three of my high school years were spent playing offensive and defensive end on our home field at Kezar Stadium. In my Senior year I earned First Team, All City honors. This attracted numerous scholarship offers from some of the country's most distinguished universities—Notre Dame, Army, and Stanford to name a few. But the college that impressed me the most was right here in my hometown—the University of San Francisco (USF). It also had something that none of the other schools could offer: a freshman football coach and one of the best recruiters I had ever met by the name of Brad Lynn.

Brad not only sold me on the exceptional academic and athletic opportunities that USF had to offer, but he also sold Mission High School's Joe Scudero and Lincoln High School's Dick Huxley as well as many other recruits from the City's high schools.

Looking back, it was the best decision I had ever made. USF gave me a strong educational foundation that molded the values I hold to this day. It also gave me the opportunity of play football on the single greatest collegiate football team ever assembled. It was my great fortune to have played with such a unique group of gifted athletes. Our 1951 undefeated and untied team speaks for itself. The camaraderie we shared on and off the field extended far beyond that of Kezar Stadium. We shared a common goal—to be better than we imagined possible; to be over-achievers not only on the playing field but academically and in life.

I want to thank my USF professors who gave me the moral guidance to face the many challenges in life and my USF coaches and teammates who will always be an integral part of my success. These were the people who helped lay the foundation for my many achievements with the San Francisco 49ers and the National Football League.

—Bob St. Clair

Bob St. Clair

BURL TOLER

After completing the fall semester of 1949 at City College of San Francisco, playing football on an undefeated team, and receiving the honor of being selected as a Junior College All American, I was still undecided about my future.

I was invited to the University of San Francisco to meet with head football coach, Joseph Kuharich, to discuss the possibility of attending the University on an athletic scholarship. The meeting was very informative and encouraging. After he gave a complete overview of the University and its programs, I was very impressed. On the spot, he offered me a scholarship and I immediately accepted the offer. The things that he said were the same things that my parents had told me before leaving my home in Tennessee for college. Some of them were:

(1) You are going to college to get an education. Play football if you wish, but get an education.
(2) Life is what YOU make it.
(3) When you graduate you will be equipped with the academic skills necessary for success in this world.
(4) You have had a Christian upbringing; don't forget what we have taught you.
(5) Do your best at everything: Remember, YOU DON'T GET something for nothing.

During the years that I was at the University, in my scholastic and athletic activities and training, all of those principles were reinforced. I have never regretted my choice, and I am proud to have had the opportunities that the University afforded me. My classes and teammates exemplify all the training and love that we were privileged to have received from the lay faculty and Jesuit fathers there. Our relations have stood the test of time.

—Burl Toler

Burl Toler

CHAPTER ONE
College Football–The 1951 Season
A Year in Review

"Produce or get out! The law of collegiate football."

—Coach Joe Kuharich
University of San Francisco
Spring Practice – 1951

1951 – Years Ago

By: Ron Fuchs

As the United States became more involved in a "police action" in a far away place called Korea, the short peace that followed World War II was at an end. Communism was rearing its ugly head in hot spots worldwide and the United States felt threatened by the spread of the totalitarian form of government. The Russians had "the bomb" and America was under threat of nuclear attack herself. That's the politics of 1951. Like most any other year, however, there was a football season to be played.

The *Army Cadets*, along with the *Fighting Irish of Notre Dame*, had dominated college football for almost a decade. The Cadets had finished second the season before behind the *Oklahoma Sooners*, who had claimed the first of three national titles under legendary head coach Bud Wilkinson. The Cadets and the Irish planned on being in the thick of things again in 1951. However, one month before the start of the season coach Earl Blaik of

Army had disaster strike his football team. Ninety cadets were caught possessing or distributing exam information and were dismissed from the proud military academy on violations of the strict honor code in place at West Point. Most of the previous season's strong squad was missing when practice began and *Army* fielded a team made up mostly of plebes (freshmen) and yearlings (sophomores). The proud Cadet program never showed up for the 1951 season, posted a 2-7-0 record, and never figured in the hunt for a third national title.

The *Irish* fared better but also did not figure in the national champioship race finishing a very average team with a 7-2-1 record, which included a 35-0 beating at the hands of the *Michigan State Spartans*.

In his next-to-last season as a coach, *Tennessee's* legendary General Robert Reese Neyland finally turned out a national champion. *Tennessee* had finished ranked second in the polls several times during Neyland's tenure in Knoxville. In 1939 they finished the regular-season undefeated, untied, and unscored on yet did not garner a title, finishing second behind an undefeated *Texas A & M* squad.

The previous year *Tennessee* fans thought they were the best team in the land after surviving the bowl games best. However, national champions were decided before the bowl games in those days and *Tennessee* finished the season ranked fourth. Fate would shine on the General and his charges in 1951 when the situation was reversed they finished the regular season ranked number one only to lose their bowl game to third-ranked *Maryland*.

Michigan State was preparing to join the tough Western Conference (now the Big 10) and coach Biggie Munn had the *Spartans* playing in championship mode. They won all their games and were in and out of the top spot in the polls throughout the year but finished second to *Tennessee* in the final AP and UPI rankings. After their lone loss the previous year the *Spartans* had won their last six games and stretched their winning streak to fifteen games by the season's end.

Michigan State football was on the verge of its best year. However, they did not look like champions much of the time during the course of the season, in six of their nine games the Spartans came from behind or broke a tie to win. Typical was the Spartans clash with the *Ohio State Buckeyes*. With ten minutes to play the *Spartans* found themselves trailing the *Buckeyes* by a 20-10 count. After closing to within three at 20-17 they pulled out the victory in the final two minutes of play, 24-20.

On the east coast Jim Tatum's *Maryland Terrapins* rolled over nine straight opponents and averaged 39.2 points per game in doing so. The thirty-nine plus points per game led the nation. The 1951 *Maryland* Terrapin football team posted the school's first undefeated and untied season. The Terrapin topped off their season, in which they finished ranked number three, with a convincing 28-13 win over top-ranked *Tennessee*.

Coach Ray Elliot had *Illinois* in the Rose Bowl for the second time in five years on New Year's Day. They were undefeated in ten games including an impressive and dominating 40-7 victory over seventh-ranked *Stanford* in Pasadena. *Stanford*, coached by Coach-of-the-Year Chuck Taylor had finished the season at 9-1-0 after losing their season-finale to *California*, 20-7. The only blot on their schedule was a 0-0 tie with *Ohio State*, now coached by Woody Hayes. The late season tie was followed by a narrow 3-0 win against *Northwestern* that clinched the Western Conference title for Illinois.

The nation's leading defense came from the Western Conference. Allowing only 154.8 yards per game and 5.9 points per game the eighth-ranked *Wisconsin Badgers* put together a 7-1-1 record. The *Badgers* only loss came in the second game of the season against Illinois. Final score: *Illinois 14, Wisconsin 10.*

Frank Gifford was in his senior season at *USC* and the big-play tailback helped lead *Southern California* to a 7-3-0 season. *USC* had started the season 7-0-0 before self-destructing and losing their last three games to *Stanford, UCLA,* and *Notre Dame.* The two conference losses versus *Stanford* and *UCLA* enabled *Stanford* to get to the Rose Bowl but the Trojans did help end the state of California's three-year unbeaten streak in the Pacific Coast Conference (now Pac10).

Mississippi's Arnold "Showboat" Boykin also ended his career in a blaze of glory. In his last game of collegiate football, in a super-human effort, Boykin scored all seven of the Rebels touchdowns, still a record, as Ole Miss leveled their in-state rival *Mississippi State Bulldogs,* 49-7.

Another Southeastern Conference team rose to the top of the class as coach Bobby Dodd's *Georgia Tech* squad finished the season ranked fifth in the nation. Tech didn't lose a game in twelve contests. Only a 14-14 tie with *Duke* blemished an otherwise perfect season for Tech. As the final moments ticked away in the Orange Bowl and a 14-14 tie with ninth-ranked *Baylor* looming on the horizon, the *Georgia Tech* defense intercepted a pass. Pepper Rodgers, who would later coach *Georgia Tech,* stepped onto the playing field and kicked a field goal that allowed Tech to escape with a 17-14 win and their eleventh victory of the year.

Heisman Trophy winner Dick Kazmaier led the *Princeton Tigers* to a sixth place finish nationally and a second straight undefeated season that ran *Princeton's* unbeaten streak to 22 games. The orange-stripped gladiators clobbered *Cornell* 53-15, *Harvard* 54-13, and *Yale* 27-0 and the Tigers were awarded the Lambert Trophy for the second year in a row as the best team in the East.

After finishing with an 8-2-1 record, the *Baylor Bears* posted their first top ten finish. *Baylor* also took undefeated *Georgia Tech* to the wire in the Orange Bowl before losing on a late field goal, 17-14.

The *San Francisco Dons* under coach Joe Kuharich had both their first perfect season and first All American in 1951. All American Ollie Matson, known as "All the way Ollie," was the nation's leading rusher with 1,566 yards on the ground, just four yards short of the collegiate record. Matson scored 21 touchdowns, one short of the 22 scored by Bobby Reynolds the previous year. His 226.3 yard average in all-purpose running made him second to the 1937 record of future Supreme Court Judge Byron "Whizzer" White of Colorado.

Oddly, after posting a perfect 9-0-0 mark, the Dons abandoned football and put the final exclamation mark on the first year of college football in the second half of the twentieth century.

*   *   *

Coach Joe Kuharich's future with the University actually began back in 1947 when he was an assistant to head coach, Ed McKeever. McKeever's style of recruiting and coaching was, what one might call, a "bit" unorthodox. After Ed's infamous "Kiss and Tell" folly, football on the Hilltop would never again be the same.

CHAPTER TWO
Gridiron Generals

"Winning isn't everything, it's the only thing."

—Washington Redskins coach,
Joe Kuharich - 1954*

Head Coach, Ed McKeever

Ed McKeever - Head Coach

USF had two very wealthy alumni, Charley Harney and Dick Parina. Harney was a contractor and future builder of Candlestick Park. Both were in the vending machine business. Needless to say, they were both very successful.

When World War II ended, they decided to *buy* the best football team that USF could afford. They recruited a former Notre Dame and Cornell University head coach by the name of Ed McKeever. His style of recruiting was on the borderline of corrupt, deceitful and underhanded, not to mention, illegal.

According to Father John Lo Schiavo, Chancellor of USF (who, in 1951, was a young scholastic and Freshman barracks Prefect), McKeever recruited potential football players out of Pennsylvania and showed them pictures of Golden Gate Park. "This is the USF campus," he would say. "Look where you are coming - you are coming to this beautiful city, this beautiful campus." But when the students arrived at the school, there was nothing but a cluster of World War II army barracks and a poor excuse for a baseball field that, in the fall, doubled as a gridiron.

Parina and Harney began paying these kids to play. Of course the money had changed hands discreetly. In other words, 'under the table'

McKeever did, however, recruit some great ball players in 1947 and 1948. "I don't recall exactly why he left," said Lo Schiavo. "If I'm not mistaken, the president of the University thought that these on-goings had gone too far or word had gotten out."

Either way, McKeever left, but not before he wrote a letter to the papers revealing all the illegal things he had done as head football coach. But that was only half of the story. He also described the University's role in this matter, and how it allowed the activities to continue. It came to be known as, "McKeever's Kiss and Tell".

*For the last 15 years, the late Vince Lombardi has been credited by historians with having proclaimed, "Winning isn't everything, it's the only thing." But according to Morris Siegel of the Washington Star, that credo was uttered as long ago as 1954 by Joe Kuharich, then in his first season as their Washington Redskins' coach. "I looked it up in the clips," Siegel says. "Joe used that line at a Redskins' welcome-home luncheon that year."

Dave Anderson, columnist
New York Times
(per the *San Francisco Chronicle*,
January 31, 1981)

THE CHARACTER BUILDER   *By Lanning*

The Evening Bulletin

PROVIDENCE, RHODE ISLAND   FRIDAY, FEBRUARY 13, 1948   PRICE FIVE CENTS

PRO GRID HEAD INCENSED OVER MCKEEVER'S ACTIONS

Excerpt from: The Evening Bulletin, Providence, Rhode Island

The football eligibility ruckus kicked up by Coach Ed McKeever at the University of San Francisco showed signs today of following him into professional football.

President Tony Morabito of the San Francisco 49ers was en route to Chicago today with demands for an investigation by the All America Conference of the "White Paper" on USF football McKeever left behind when he became coach of the Chicago Rockets.

> After coaching the USF Dons for a year, McKeever abruptly resigned last month to take the pro team job and wrote a widely circulated letter in which he questioned eligibility of 22 USF players and money paid to some of the Dons.

Morabito left last night for a weekend meeting of officials of the All America Conference, of which the 49ers and Rockets are members. "I'll say plenty about this at the meeting", Morabito said. He said he considered McKeever's action "my business and I don't like it." "We're trying to build good will- not tear it down. He is one of us and people can't help but ask, "What kind of coaches do you hire?"

University of San Francisco officials meanwhile returned a heavy fire of counter charges at McKeever and coaches of other schools to whom McKeever sent copies of his letter that made caustic comments-.

USF athletic officials charged McKeever had:

1. Told five players he brought here for the Don team to cover up the fact they had previously attended other colleges.

2. Stripped the athletic files of such papers as schedule negotiations, alumni letters on prospects and football plans.

3. Repeatedly exceeded budgets for grid games, including $4200 spent instead of the $2500 allowed for the Loyola game in Los Angeles.

> The Rev. Jerome Sullivan, USF athletic moderator, announced only one of the 22 players named by McKeever, Phil O'Connor, formerly of Notre Dame and St. Louis University—definitely was ineligible. Only one other—Joe Mocha, said by McKeever to have attended Pittsburgh, Bethany and Maryland— remains in doubt, Father Sullivan said.

He added that McKeever had "compromised" the five players who failed to mention previous college attendance, but that their names will be cleared unless any opponent objects to their playing.

Coach Lynn Waldorf of California today added his voice to the criticism of McKeever's action by several western athletic officials.

"It must have been a deep seated, violent feud to have caused him to act like that," Waldorf said. He termed it "deserting his own kids."

Other criticism came from Coach Jimmy Phelan of St. Mary's, Athletic Director, Brutus Hamilton of California and Coach Leonard Casanova of Santa Clara.

Phelan, president of the American Football Coaches' Association, said he removed McKeever from the AFCA's radio committee. He called McKeever's action "highly unethical and a breach of common decency."

Phelan replaced McKeever on the committee with Joe Kuharich, his successor as USF coach.

* * *

USF Coaching Staff: Bob Maddock, Robert MacKenzie,
Ed McKeever, and Joe Kuharich

Joe Kuharich - Head Coach

"He didn't talk a lot and rarely said anything stronger than 'hell' or 'damn,' but when he did, the grass stood on end!" said '51 team backup quarterback, Bill Henneberry.

Joseph Lawrence Kuharich was born to be in football. He came into this world on April 14, 1917, in South Bend, Indiana where, as a youngster, he and his friends would sneak into Notre Dame games at the old Cartier field through a broken wooden plank. This became a regular Saturday ritual - that is to say until that one infamous Saturday afternoon. As Joe crawled through the broken board, he was met on the other side by none other than Knute Rockne, the legendary Notre Dame coach.

Head Coach, Joe Kuharich

"Rockne told me to stand aside," Kuharich said. "He waited for my four pals to crawl through, one by one, and then he made us crawl back through the fence. But then he told us, "I don't want you boys doing this any more. If you want to go to a game, meet me at 11 o'clock outside the main gate and I'll take you in with me."

USF was Kuharich's first job as a head coach, but he had already established a solid 'football education' at Notre Dame before arriving at the Hilltop as an assistant coach in 1947. Kuharich was not only an outstanding student, but also an outstanding guard for the Fighting Irish from 1935 through 1937. He was rated as one of the best in the country and was named All American. Joe was a member of the 1938 College All Star team that defeated the NFL's Washington Redskins 28-16 at Soldier's Field in Chicago.

Following the 1937 season, the Pittsburgh Steelers drafted Kuharich, but he elected to stay on at Notre Dame as Freshman coach for the 1938 season.

In 1939, Joe accepted the head coaching position at Vincentian Institute in Albany, New York. While enjoying a winning season at Vincentian, the Steelers traded their rights to him to the Brooklyn Dodgers. The coach of the Dodgers was none other than Dr. John Bain (Jock) Sutherland. Realizing how far he would be from home, Joe requested that he be traded to the Chicago Cardinals in order to be closer to South Bend. His request was granted and in 1940 he was traded to the Cardinals.

Head coach Jim Conzelman played Joe as a starting right guard (a position he held throughout the 1940 and 1941 seasons). Conzelman was so impressed with Kuharich's profound knowledge of football that he bestowed upon him the unprecedented responsibility for calling both the offensive and defensive signals! In 1941 Joe was named first string All Pro, even though his team finished in last place.

From 1942 through 1944, Kuharich served as a lieutenant in the Navy, and in 1946, retired from professional football. He accepted the line coaching position with the Steelers that was offered to him by Sutherland. This was the only time that a non-Pittsburgh man was ever hired as an assistant under Sutherland's reign. The following season Kuharich began his coaching career with the University of San Francisco as the Dons' line coach, and in 1948, upon McKeever's resignation, was offered the position of head coach. And with this new era of USF football, the annals of the history of collegiate football were about to be rewritten.

Kuharich was a taskmaster on the practice field. "Joe was nicknamed by his players, 'The Barracuda', because if you made a mistake or you weren't really hustling, he'd just eat you up!" recalled end Bob St. Clair.

"He was tough," said right halfback Bill Dando.

"He had a high-pitched voice that would let you know how much trouble you were in if you messed up!" recalled center Larry Slajchert.

Defensive lineman Vince Tringali remembered, "I was so afraid of that man, I couldn't ever get up the nerve to say, "hello." I'd developed a stutter just trying to talk to him."

During spring practice, Joe proved to be an extremist about conditioning and fundamentals. According to fullback Roy Giorgi, "Kuharich was a tyrant on the football field. When he yelled you could hear him all over the field."

Despite the fact that he looked up to and respected the great Knute Rockne, his locker room speeches were little to be desired. "Produce or get out!" Kuharich would tell his players. "It's the law of collegiate football." But he was also gifted when it came to instilling in them a sense of loyalty, (both to him and to each other) that would extend far beyond the playing field.

"He taught me that hard work, being honest with yourself and others, and treating all people equally will make you a good person," said guard Dick Columbini.

Kuharich was thirty-four years old in 1951 - his fourth year as the USF football coach. He delegated his recruiting responsibilities to the freshman coach, Brad Lynn. All Lynn could offer his prospective players in the way of scholarship incentives was tuition, room and board. Pete Rozelle, the school's athletic news director, praised Lynn for recruiting so many great players. "Brad would take the recruits to our highest hill with a good view of San Francisco. "That, he would say, is your campus."

USF football was experiencing some deep financial problems in 1951. The sport was costing the Jesuits approximately $70,000 a year - a cost that they could no longer afford. Another Bay Area Catholic college, St. Mary's, proved that the sport was too costly, therefore, dropped football after the 1950 season. Gate receipts were the major moneymakers for football, but since the arrival of the San Francisco 49ers professional football team in 1946, attendance at games in Kezar Stadium had declined by nearly 80 percent.

Football powerhouses, Cal (U. C. Berkeley) and Stanford, were major competition for USF. Under coach Pappy Waldorf, Cal made the trip to the Rose Bowl in 1949 and 1950 (Stanford would not make it until 1952.). Both the Bears and the Indians had played - and defeated - the '50 team, but were well aware of the talent that the Dons would field in '51. And at the chance of being beaten by the considerably stronger 51 team (and there was a good chance that could happen) the risk of embarrassment was too close for comfort.

"Teams were wary of us, and rightfully so. After all, there was no sense in playing us. If they lost or came close to losing to a little school like us, they would lose a lot of prestige," said defensive tackle, Gino Marchetti.

Therefore, Kuharich was left to come up with a patchwork schedule. This included two games with one school, San Jose State, and two more with service teams, the Camp Pendleton Marines and the San Diego Naval Training Center. Neither, though loaded with former pro and college players, was much of a drawing card. Idaho didn't exactly pack in the stadium, either. The only teams on USF's schedule that year that were recognized as high-attendance draws were Fordham, Santa Clara, College of the Pacific and Loyola of Los Angeles. Both Fordham and Loyola had gone 8-1 in 1950, and Pacific had high-profile players in quarterback Doug Scovil and future Chicago Bear's halfback Eddie Macon.

So, in reality, the problem with the 51 season was not so much winning games as it was getting people to attend them. The football program's financial situation desperately needed to get into the black. This monumental task was placed on the shoulders of athletic news director Rozelle. Pete, along with USF play-by-play reporter and best friend, Mike De Long, would supply the sports reporters with all the necessary information about the team that was needed for the foundation of their stories. Pete and Mike would personally visit each and every one of the city's four major newspapers. Rozelle wanted the team to receive as much media exposure as possible. The more exposure, the better the draw.

Kuharich knew he had the talent to post his third straight winning season. He knew this back in 1949 when the team was first brought together; but no one - not the coaches, the players, or the fans could have predicted how really good they would become.

Line Coach Bud Kerr, Coach Kuharich, and Backfield Coach Jim Ryan.

The Coaching Staff

James C. Ryan - Backfield Coach

Former USF quarterback standout Jim Ryan served his second season as the Dons' backfield coach.

The twenty-five year old Ryan was born on March 21, 1926 and attended St. Mary's High in Berkeley, California. Jim excelled in football, basketball and baseball.

As a freshman starter on the 1946 varsity squad, Ryan lettered all four years and achieved an outstanding passing record. In four seasons he

WILLIAM (BUD) KERR
LINE COACH

JAMES C. RYAN
BACKFIELD COACH

BRAD LYNN
FRESHMAN COACH

EUGENE (SCRAP IRON) YOUNG
TRAINER

completed 145 passes in 330 attempts for 2310 yards and 19 touchdowns. Upon graduation at USF, Jim accrued the Boyle Award, as the school's outstanding senior athlete.

Coach Ryan proved to be a valuable addition to the USF coaching staff. During the 1951 season while under his command the talented Don backs compiled their most impressive offensive record in the annals of USF football history.

Bradley "Brad" Lynn - Freshman Coach and Recruiter

Born Bradley Nicholas Lynn on January 26, 1917, in Santa Cruz, California, he was one of three Notre Dame men on the Don coaching staff. Brad attended Santa Cruz High School and San Mateo Junior College, where he lettered in football, basketball, and track.

He transferred to Notre Dame as a junior and played on the varsity football team from 1936 to 1939. He graduated with a Bachelor's degree in history.

After serving on the coaching staff at Arizona State in 1940, Lynn entered the Navy and served six years as a lieutenant. He saw action at the Battle of Leyte Gulf.

During 1946 and 1947 he turned in one of the finest prep coaching records in the State. His Santa Cruz High School Seahawks compiled an unprecedented 15-2 record.

In 1950 Lynn worked with the varsity backs and tutored the freshmen. In 1951 he worked exclusively with the USF freshmen squad.

William (Bud) Howard Kerr - Line Coach

William "Bud" Kerr was born in Tarrytown, New York, on November 10, 1915. Although he had never played high school football, he earned first team, All American honors at Notre Dame as an end in 1939. He graduated from the South Bend campus in 1940, and played in both the East-West and College All Star games of that year.

Bud played professionally with the Los Angeles Dons in 1946 before serving as a line coach at Denver University in 1947 and 1948. He arrived at USF in the spring of 1949, where he had experienced much success as the Dons' line coach. Kerr's knowledge and expertise allowed USF to be ranked fourth in the nation in 1950 by holding opponents to an average rushing gain of 74.5 yards per game.

Eugene "Scrap Iron" Young - Head Trainer

The Dons' head trainer, Eugene "Scrap Iron" Young, was one of the most widely known men in his profession. He had been associated with athletic teams as a trainer for the past twenty-six years.

In 1923 "Scrap Iron" began his career as trainer while still an undergraduate at Notre Dame. For the next twenty-three years Young remained with the Fighting Irish through its Golden Era in football. Beginning under the reign of the immortal Knute Rockne, his tenure at Notre Dame spanned grid coaching dominance from "Hunk" Anderson to Frank Leahey. But the nickname, 'Scrap Iron,' came from Rockne, himself. He was impressed with the aggressiveness that Young had portrayed as a lineman while playing freshman football. In 1927 Young graduated with a degree in law from Notre Dame.

In 1946 the Detroit Lions' hired Scrap Iron as their trainer. In 1947 he began work with the Chicago Rockets.

1950 was Young's first year on the Hilltop. With the winning sports tradition that prevailed at Notre Dame while he was there, USF experienced its finest athletic success in history as its basketball, tennis, soccer, and rifle teams all won championships.

In 1951, Young left the University for the private sector. He was replaced by Frank Zanazzi.

Athletic Administration Staff

Dick Domino - Head Manager

Dick came to USF in 1948 from Brawley Union High School in Brawley, California on a football scholarship. While playing end in his freshman year, he broke his jaw which abruptly ended his football career. His playing days over, Coach Kuharich recruited him as an assistant manager in 1949, taking over the head manager duties in 1950. The popular Dons' manager received his USF degree in 1953.

Pete Rozelle - Athletic Publicity Director

Pete Rozell was born on March 1, 1926, in South Gate, California. He attended Compton High School and Compton Junior College. At Compton J. C., he played basketball and established Compton's first athletic news bureau.

His publicity efforts at Compton were noted by Dons' basketball coach Pete Newell, and in 1948 Rozelle transferred to USF and became the Athletic Publicity Director.

After his graduation in 1950, Pete continued working at the University, promoting USF athletics until 1952.

To prepare you for Kuharich's 'old school' techniques in training and discipline, we will first have to return to training camp, August 1950. As Joe Kuharich began searching for the perfect training site, he had three things in mind: intense heat, little or no shade, and total desolation. He found that perfect place in Corning, California.

3
CHAPTER THREE
Camp Kuharich

Rancho Tehama (Camp Kuharich) – Corning, California (1950)

"When I think of Corning, I think of being in the middle of a desert, with no water, and a little man yelling at you for six hours a day. Without a doubt, those were the roughest two weeks of my career."

—Tackle Gino Marchetti
Spring Training, 1950

At a time when most college coaches were moving their spring practices to cooler environments, Joe Kuharich was scanning the countryside in pursuit of a hot weather site for his intensive two-week conditioning program for his USF players. In August of 1950 the remote town of Corning, California was designated as the perfect locale. The grueling workouts in the 115-degree heat combined with Kuharich's passion for "old school" fundamentals and conditioning would prevail in the minds of these players for more than fifty years.

"There was nothing there except the field," recalled Bob St. Clair. "No trees, no buildings, no shade. There was one telephone pole. If we'd get even a few minutes' break, ten guys would line up single file to get the shade from that pole. Joe Scudero (5'9") was the smartest guy on our team; he'd line up behind me (6'8")."

"That was my first real introduction to football the way it was done in the Midwest," continued St. Clair. "It was so damn hot out there, you really had to dig down deep and pull on whatever guts you had."

On the other hand, you could try to get out of practice, as did offensive lineman Vince Tringali.

"I figured the only way out of the torture was to leave practice and the only way to do that was to get knocked out," he said. "So I had a plan that I was gonna knock myself out. I started running into people and hitting the hell out of them. I got very dizzy, but never knocked out. The guys even started complimenting me on all my good hits. I said, 'Forget the hits, damnit, I wanna get knocked out!'"

In order to keep their name on the roster, players would have to endure the tortuous training methods of Kuharich. One of the more brutal drills took place in what the players called The Pit. This was designed by Kuharich, himself. The Pit was created by first setting up a couple of lightly padded railroad ties. Once the ties were in place, players were forced to squeeze between them and battle each other, one on one, gladiator style.

Fullback Dick Huxley remembers, "Corning was Hell!! Joe's work ethic was insane. We had turned into animals."

Spring Training, 1950 (Corning, California)

San Francisco Chronicle

The City's Only Home-Owned Newspaper

FOUNDED 1865   SAN FRANCISCO. MONDAY, SEPTEMBER 3, 1950   GA 1-1112

Don Gridders Have Found A Liking for Straw Hats And Large Corning Olives

By: Will Connolly

CORNING, Sept. 3 - Thank goodness the Maywood Hotel where the University of San Francisco footballers are being quartered, has shower baths. The boys would be afraid to use tub baths, lest they go down the drain when the plug was pulled.

That's how attenuated they feel. As already reported on the first day, Dick Colombini, guard from Santa Rosa, dropped 11 pounds. His was not an isolated example. Bob St. Clair, 6 foot 7 stringbean end, lost 12 pounds on his spare frame and Mike Mergen, sophomore tackle from McHenry, Ill., shed 13.

But the champ seems to be Guard Dick Stanfel of San Francisco. In two days he came out 18 pounds lighter.

"I was 238 when I checked in and now I'm 220," groused Stanfel. "These pants were tight around the waist. Look, they're flapping around on me."

Quarterback Ed Brown likewise is going around in baggy pants. "I used to fasten my belt on the second hole," he said. "Now I use the fifth."

Coach Joe Kuharich was unimpressed. Like all Notre Damers he had a story to top anything the USFers told.

Weighty Tale

"Ten or 15 pounds in one day - what's that? Why, when I was at Notre Dame we had a tackle from Detroit named Art Cronin. He was a wealthy kid and didn't have to work during the summer. The first day of practice he lost 21 pounds. That's right, 21!"

The losses would indicate the boys are not in shape but Coach Kuharich contends this is not true. On the whole, they reported in the pink of fine fettle - better than he's ever seen them - he said.

Then why the great drop in poundage? No muscle or tissue is being lost. Kuharich explained. Simply water weight through the pores. The lads will regain that after drinking a few gallons of iced tea, which is the favorite beverage up here, even ahead of carbonated drinks.

The first day, last Friday, was uncommonly hot even for this olive-growing community. Olives are supposed to require 90 days of 100-degree temperature to mature, and the USFers don't doubt it. Friday was 110 downtown and on the high school field probably 115. Saturday and today were practically the same, perhaps a degree or two cooler.

Gripes Galore

At first, the USFers griped after the manner of ex-GI's.

"I don't get it," grumbled Roy Barni, "Chico State, near here, moves away to escape the heat and we come up to get it."

But the footballers really don't mean it. They're getting acclimated. The turf, equipment and other facilities at Union High School are of the best and the boys love that swimming pool. Townspeople are hospitable. Every afternoon after practice great bowls of iced olives are placed in the hotel lobby for the USFers to munch on. The things are as big as lemons, darn near.

The first evening the squad got away with two gallons of black olives so the ration was increased to four gallons or all they want. Imagine the luxury of eating olives until they come out of your ears?

Frank Morgan, owner of an olive orchard and prune dehydrator, made the USFers feel a little better by offering them the use of his plant for conditioning themselves. It seems the temperature inside the dehydrator is 165 degrees and men work in it - two at a time in case one keels over.

"If you fellows want, you can warm up in the dehydrator, then dash out on the field and freeze," Morgan volunteered.

Salt Tablets

He had no takers,

Art Alois, center, who spent the summer working in an ice cream plant, and Harold Sachs, another center, who was life guard at a San Clemente pool, yearned for the good old days.

Trainer Scrap Iron Young is feeding the lads four salt tablets a day. In San Francisco, he'd give them one if the day was uncommonly warm, but usually none.

The gridders have an hour of leisure after lunch. Some retire to their rooms for a nap, others stroll the streets. Most of those who venture outdoors wear 59-cent farmer's straw hats, which they purchased here. The gals along Fulton street back home would be proud of the rakish angles by which the likes of Ken McNulty, Whizzer White, Ollie Matson, Roy Barni, Dick Huxley, Bob Weibel, and George Carley wear their high-crown straws.

But the day is well filled with scheduled events and there is little leisure. Here is a day in the life of a USFer while he's here:

7:00 a.m.	Out of the sack
7:30	Mass
8:00	Breakfast
8:45	Lecture or skill practice
9:45 - 11:15	Field work
12:15	Lunch
2:30	Meeting and lecture
3:30 - 5:30	Field work
6:45	Dinner
8:00	Lecture or game movies
10:15	Bed check, room by room, by Trainer Young.

The coaching staff has no trouble with the young men after dark. They're all so tired that they drag their bones upstairs to bed as soon as the post-dinner meeting is over. Seven comes awfully early.

It develops that this department was indirectly responsible for the Dons coming to Corning. Weeks ago, we wrote that Coach Kuharich was looking for a nice warm spot to train. Right away, Estil Clark, soda fountain and newsstand owner and member of the Corning Chamber of Commerce, took pen in hand and described the beauties of this Tehama county town to Kuharich. Joe came up, looked around, and the deal was made.

Booster Clark saw it first in The Chronicle.

Apart from the warmth here and the fact that USF's dining hall on the Hilltop is currently being repaired, training for ten days out of town has another advantage, according to Kuharich.

"USF is a day school," he reminded. "Twenty of our players live at home. They're scattered all over the city. They don't have much of a chance to know one another socially. During practice, the linemen are at one end of the field, the backs at another. But here they can have social relations in the lobby."

That is, if they can find time.

*   *   *

The players, those who survived, will never forget Corning. This is what a few of the 'survivers' had to say when asked to relive their time in 'Hell'.

Center Hal Sachs - "Corning was hot, I mean really hot. Made this Atheist believe he was preparing for his final destination, because of the number of poor choices to that point.... like being here. Corning was the pits. Let's face it, their main crop was olives. Have not been able to look an olive in the face since 1950. We all bought straw hats and everyone added their personal touch in an attempt to be the most dapper. After all, it was the only shade in town."

Guard Dick Stanfel - "Corning. Hardest and toughest training camp I have ever gone through. When you tell people about the stories, they don't believe you. No air conditioning. No water on the field. One telephone pole for shade – players lined up. The heat got to you. You became mean. You wanted to hurt people. Conditions were so terrible. Four to five in a room. One shower for everyone. On the field for two to three hours. The food was just adequate. We had some battles."

End Ed Dawson - "Corning has a very special place in my heart! During the days, the time on the practice field seemed to go on and on and on. The temperature was so hot that we were dying for water. Joe decided that we should not be drinking very much water and to prevent us from doing this, he put oatmeal in the water pail so that you could only wash out your mouth - not drink. So, we started drinking the water off of the grass in the end zones. That lasted only for one day as Joe instructed the groundskeepers to only water the grass after we were through for the day; that way, the water would have time to seep into the ground by the time we returned to practice the next day. Then Scrap Iron Young came up with a great solution. He informed us that if you consumed a beer, it would not only give you increased energy, but it also helped quench your thirst. Therefore, several of us, after each practice, would run to the store and down one beer as quickly as possible. We always made sure that the best players on the team, Ollie, Burl, Gino or Ed was with us (not that they needed much encouragement) so that if Joe smelled beer on our breath, he might not do something too drastic to us. The only problem with the beer was that when you were tired...exhausted, and downed the beer, you got a little buzz; as a result, we always tried to sit as far away from Joe and the other coaches as possible."

"The hotel rooms did not have any type of air conditioning and as a result, you could not get to sleep. I can remember taking my pillow and going down to the lobby and sleeping on the marble floor, and it worked!"

End Ralph Thomas - "Corning training camp personified Joe's work ethic. It really was the acid test for all of us and it certainly was not for the faint of heart. None of us had ever experienced this type of oppressive heat. I do believe, however, that we all drew strength from each other like survivors in a natural disaster who bond together. We became the leanest, meanest, best-conditioned football machine that maybe ever played the game."

Guard Dick Colombini - (in a joking manner on Kuharich moving him from fullback to guard) "It was a great opportunity. I changed from being behind Matson to being behind Stanfel!"

End Bob St. Clair - "Joe was a real taskmaster. From the old Notre Dame school of football. He erected a platform scaffold where he would stand during practice with a megaphone and bark out criticisms and praises. He was extremely excitable. A Vince Lombardi/Knute Rockne type of personality."

Fullback Ollie Matson - "I went up there (to Corning) weighing 210 pounds and came back weighing 188. But I was ready!"

Guard Lou "Red" Stephens - "When we talk about Corning, we sort of have to list it as fiction. After all, who runs 100-yard wind sprints and scrimmages when it's 110 to 120 degrees? I don't know if I was fortunate or unfortunate. I missed about half of the training sessions because of an injury."

*   *   *

When those two weeks in Hades finally came to a close, the players were anxious to get back home. Those who were native San Franciscans returned to their homes in the City. For those who were recruited from other cities and states, home was "the barracks."

CHAPTER FOUR
The Barracks

"The first thing we saw when we drove on campus was the Barracks."
Coach said, "This is where you'll be living."
We said, "You've got to be kidding!"

—Halfback Bill Dando - 1950

San Francisco Chronicle
The City's Only Home-Owned Newspaper

SAN FRANCISCO   DECEMBER 30, 1977

A WILD BUNCH
Party Times on the Hilltop
By: Bruce Jenkins, Chronicle Sportswriter

To hear the players reflect on USF in the early 1950's, it becomes apparent that the Dons enjoyed a good time at least as much as a victory.

"It was a great combination of people," Vince Tringali recalls. "We had some real quiet, studious guys like Burl Toler and Ralph Thomas, but we had some completely crazy ones - Marchetti, St. Clair, Ed Brown, Joe Scudero, Roy Barni...we're dealing with men here, not boys. I was a little nuts, too, believe me. We did some things you can't print."

Brown remembers the players as "loose. Definitely free swingers. Joe (Kuharich) had his rules, and we weren't about to get away with anything when he was around. But we enjoyed ourselves."

"Ed has settled down now," says Tringali. "But he was a wild man in those days. Great passer that he was, he'd get on Kuharich's nerves sometimes and Joe would bench him. Later on, I'd go watch Ed play for the Bears when they came to Kezar. George Halas (then the Chicago coach) thought I was a sex pervert hanging around their bench in my overcoat. He didn't trust anybody Ed Brown knew."

Some of the goings-on in the campus barracks — where many of the players lived — were, let's say, out of the ordinary. "You can imagine some of the stuff that went on," says Bob St. Clair. "It was all part of the tremendous camaraderie we had. We enjoyed every minute."

"John McKay was at USF," Tringali said, "for about three days. He was recruited, came there and said he wanted out. He was gonna blow the whistle on the guys who weren't going to class, so the school gave him a ticket and sent him back to West Virginia." (Later, Tringali would send several of his St. Ignatius High players to USC under McKay, and the two are now close friends.)

"We never had any racial problems," Tringali said, "and that was the real key to our success. We'd stand up for Burl and Ollie Matson any time — though they could take care of themselves."

Five members at a USF Hall of Fame banquet in 1970: From left, Coach Joe
Kuharich, Pete Rozelle, Bob St. Clair, Burl Toler, and Ralph Thomas.

"When we played the Camp Pendleton Marines in '51, some of them started
popping off to Ollie, calling him down. So he simply started breaking bones.
Clean tackles, mind you, but he was sending them out of the game one by one.
Chopped 'em right off their feet. That ended that crap in a hurry."

Matson says, "after playing at USF, with everybody pulling together, it
was a real shock for me in the pros. I couldn't believe guys could be on the
same team, yet be so distant. We had a loyalty and a closeness you just don't
find any more."

*   *   *

Players who were from "the City" and the surrounding areas lived at home
while attending USF. The other players lived on campus in what was known as
"The Barracks." These were 'Quonset huts' on the USF campus that were built
by the Army during World War II, and left behind after the war had ended.
They were not in the greatest of shape. Some days the heat would be on full
blast; other days there would be no heat at all. On top of that, the roof leaked.

There were six barracks in all. Three of the barracks were used to house
the athletes. There were fifty students in each barrack - about one hundred
and fifty altogether. One of the barracks was for the Jesuits; another housed

the dining room and kitchen, and the other was the locker room and training room. Athletes from all sports were mixed together. Father John Lo Schiavo was in charge of freshmen football players in one barracks.

"Freshmen were already unruly enough - and that's if they were normal. But when you were dealing with All City and All State football players from cities such as Chicago, Pennsylvania, Milwaukee, and Omaha, they truly believed that they were at USF as God's gift to San Francisco," Lo Schiavo said. "Especially the kids from Chicago. They considered themselves to be the 'sophisticates' of the group."

Center Larry Slajchert – "The Barracks were an experience one would never forget. There was absolutely no privacy and as freshmen, we enjoyed harassing Fr. John LoSchiavo who was our Prefect and a scholastic at that time. (A Prefect was the overseer of a barrack(s) – a cross between a guard and a housemother). It wasn't till later years that I realized the burden he carried. He was a student as well as a teacher and in charge of a group of misfits out of control. Somehow he survived."

Guard Dick Colombini – "There was a Filipino student who was assigned, by mistake, to the football players' dorm. He wanted to decorate his entrance and installed drapes over the front door – which were promptly set on fire. The fire was extinguished and, needless to say, he was transferred to another barracks."

Athletic Publicist Pete Rozelle – "We would play hearts in the barracks until all hours of the night. Whoever got nailed with the queen of spades would set off a screaming match to the point where our Prefect, Father (Herman) Hauck (later president of the University of Santa Clara), would have to come and quiet us down."

Guard Lou Stephens – "There are many stories about the barracks and probably most of them are true. One of my roommates was 'Frenchy' from Chicago, who told me he didn't like clean sheets. After six weeks I believed him and took over the 'bedding brigade'. But all in all, the barracks were fun. We rarely had a Prefect, so it was pretty free and easy. Surprisingly enough, nobody abused this lack of supervision very much – we were all too tired after running the whole practice.

In our senior year, our Prefect did decide to enforce the curfew. We instituted rallies, parades, and whatever in front of his room. It took about two weeks and he moved back to the priests' quarters. We were again free to ignore any time limits."

End Ed Dawson – "Being young and always hungry, we used to try and cook food in our rooms and our Prefect was always trying to find out which room contained the restaurant for that particular night. However, since the rooms were all on the ground floor, we could sneak the food out the window while delaying the Prefect from entering the room. Our stove was an electric double burner. We had one or two pans and, if you wanted toast, we had an old metal clothes hanger that had been bent into a shape that held the bread over one of the burners.

I remember we had a couple of guys from Chicago. One of them was a quarterback and his favorite relaxation was to dress up like Zorro (including a sword, mask and cape), run up and down the halls 'defending the weak and those unable to defend themselves'. Every once in a while he would get someone to 'fence' with him and that really turned him on!"

Center Hal Sachs – "The barracks basically were bleak, barren, and bone-ass ugly. Nevertheless, they soon became home. My roommate was Ed Dawson, also from Southern California, so we had beach talk in common and he had a great collection of Stan Kenton's tunes. We got along well, except he always had dates. I was broke and had a girl at home. I resigned myself to the facts of poverty.

Both Ed and I, being beach people, attempted to attract every stray sunray possible from the usually cloud-shrouded hilltop called home. This particular day, we were blessed with more sun than usual. Postponing suiting up for practice as long as possible, Ed and I removed our T-shirts and sat on the bench outside our barracks when, lo and behold, down the road came 'T' Texas Toler, loose as a goose. We extended an invitation to join us. He removed his T-shirt, sat on the bench between us and stretched out to a full reclining position. After no more than five seconds, he jumped to his feet and poking at his belly said, "Oh, my goodness, I'm turning pink. I gotta go see Scrap Iron and get some lotion!"

"He got such a kick out of himself, he let go with that infectious Toler cackle."

End Ralph Thomas – "In the off-season of our senior year, 'nameless' had been out on the town and obviously had more than enough. When he tried to maneuver his '35 Chevy down the street leading to our barracks, he missed the turn and ploughed into the priests' barracks at the top of the hill. The car was still there the next morning when we got up for breakfast and we never knew what 'nameless' told the priest whose bedroom his car crashed into."

The men of the barracks have innumerable stories to tell but only few are fit to print.

Whether they lived in the barracks or lived at home, they all had one common goal: to be the best college team ever. And why not? With players like Brown, Marchetti, Matson and Toler, how could you lose?

Kuharich shared that same goal with his team. When the media began asking questions about his '51 squad, Joe didn't pull any punches.

5
CHAPTER FIVE
Headlines—USF

"Togetherness proved to be our biggest strength. When you're united; when you're together like we were and respected one another like we did, you're awfully hard to beat."

—Fullback Ollie Matson - 1951

USF PROSPECTUS - 1951

The *1951 USF Football Media Guide* had this to say about the Hilltop's powerful, varsity squad:

"Blessed with four of the finest senior football players in America as the nucleus of a veteran squad, USF should field one of its top teams in history for 1951. Head coach, Joe Kuharich, will have 20 lettermen back in the fold, plus several promising sophs up from a frosh squad that dropped only one game. Most of the regulars launched their varsity collegiate careers on the Hilltop in 1949 and saw considerable action on the club that won seven of ten games that season and came back with a 7-4 record in '50."

Although the limelight will be shared with the rest of this talented squad, it's predicted that the caliber of this 24-carat quartet - fullback, Ollie Matson, quarterback, Ed Brown, left tackle, Gino Marchetti and linebacker, Burl Toler, will be the power and strength behind this team. Leading the running attack will be 203-pound fullback, Ollie Matson. With his power and capacity for speed, Matson is a strong threat both inside or outside as well as in pass receiving. In the past two years, Matson's stats have tallied for 20 touchdowns and an impressive 1600 yards rushing. This may be Matson's year to make All-American.

Quarterback, Ed Brown is expected to give quite an aerial show this year. Last season he connected 59 times in 140 attempts for a total of 1205 yards and 10 touchdowns. Senior ends, Merrill Peacock and Ralph Thomas as well as junior end, Bob St. Clair have been the Hilltop's most prominent receivers. Last season they caught 43 passes for a combined total of 826 yards. Brown's versatility on the gridiron has deemed him the Dons' punter. Ranking fourth in the nation in 1949, he averaged 42.7 yards per kick. Last year he booted 60 for an average of 37.1 yards with three blocked kicks. Brown will also be responsible for the point after conversions while Matson will execute the kick off.

Left tackle Gino Marchetti and linebacker Burl Toler will fortify and protect the line. Both were All Coast selections in 1950. Marchetti is expected to be one of the nation's finest tackles this season. At six foot three inches, Gino tips the scales at 225 pounds, and is extremely fast and aggressive. Excluding ends, he is USF's fastest lineman. Toler has been an offensive end, linebacker and offensive tackle. At six feet two inches and 210 pounds he is considered to be a vicious tackler. Burl is expected to earn an array of individual honors before moving into a professional football career with the Cleveland Browns who have drafted him for their 1952 season.

Other standouts: The left halfback position will be filled by Joe Scudero replacing graduate Roy Barni. Scudero scored 9 touchdowns as a sophomore in 1950. Center Hal Sachs will fill the void left by graduating senior, Al Alois, and sophomore guards, John Dwyer and Bob Schaeffer, are expected to replace Dick Stanfel, the outstanding guard who was recently chosen for the All Star game in Chicago, and is the Detroit Lions' number one draft choice.

Spring practice uncovered an effective backup for Brown in quarterback Bill Henneberry, who is also USF's newly elected student body president. Other talents include senior halfbacks, George Carley and Vince Sakowski. Fullbacks Roy Giorgi and Dick Huxley, and halfback Jim Kearney are also expected to see more action this year.

According to the 1951 USF Football Media Guide, "Kuharich will continue his version of the "T" formation - a combination of the Notre Dame "T", Cross "T" and "K" formations. He contemplates utilizing more flankers, however, to give Brown's passing greater emphasis."

It has recently come to the attention of USF that pro scouts have been observing five Dons, something even the talented Cal Bears could not claim. Brown, Matson, Marchetti, Toler and St. Clair are expected shoe-ins to be drafted by the pros.

Dick Friendlich, Chronicle staff writer, had this to say in an article he wrote in May of 1950. "The Dons looked so dangerous that three Pacific Coast Conference teams looking for games passed them by in favor of open dates or somebody else. If a bettor were called upon to wager right now on USF's chances against each foe, the Dons would undoubtedly be solid favorites in four games with certainly no worse than even money in the remaining four. Today, that is. October could be something else again. But the undefeated season is no mere dream."

Practice – wind sprints – USF field

San Francisco Foghorn

OFFICIAL PUBLICATION OF THE ASSOCIATED STUDENTS

UNIVERSITY OF SAN FRANCISCO

SAN FRANCISCO, APRIL 6, 1951

Kuharich Slates Team Scrimmage After 1st Week of Spring Drills

By: Al Schlarmann

Sixty-five athletes jogged onto the practice field last Monday afternoon to begin training for next fall's grid campaign. Head Coach Joe Kuharich describes this year's squad as the best of his three-year coaching reign and is looking forward to a successful practice session. This is the first time that the staff cannot concentrate on 10 or 15 men because there are no more real football players than that on the squad. This spring Kuharich has from 30 to 40 men with real football ability and others who show great promise.

The big weakness of the team is offensive blocking. The success of the Dons' scoring ability depends on how rapidly line coach Bud Kerr can teach his men to block correctly. The center of the Green and Gold forward wall is somewhat weak because of inadequate reserves at the tackle and guard slots.

With the exception of Roy Barni who graduated, USF will field the same backfield as last season. Joe Scudero, Vince Sakowski and George Carley make up the nucleus of a crew of fleet, experienced halfbacks. Last year's reserves and a small crop of junior college transfers will provide some relief, but it is still too early to single out the individuals.

Dick Huxley, a shifty power back, has shown the greatest improvement to date, and with a little more experience could fill the gap left by Barni.

Ollie Matson is still the fastest man on the team, which he proved by covering the hundred in 10.5 seconds with full equipment. Free of the injuries which plagued him through most of last season, Ollie is ready to prove that his is one of the best backs on the Coast.

End play, which was one of the big headaches of 1950, should be much better this fall. Merrill Peacock is a fine receiver and promises to revert back to his 1949 form. 6 foot 7 inch Bob St. Clair has developed some of the poise necessary to make him one of the outstanding ends on the team.

Ed Brown, the team's passing specialist, will run the offensive machine from the quarterback position. With a greater emphasis on passing, Ed will be more of a threat than ever before.

Contact work has been in progress all week and a scrimmage has been scheduled for tomorrow.

*   *   *

Toler, Brown, Marchetti, and Matson

𝔖𝔞𝔫 𝔍𝔯𝔞𝔫𝔠𝔦𝔰𝔠𝔬 𝔈𝔵𝔞𝔪𝔦𝔫𝔢𝔯

Monarch of the Dailies

SATURDAY, SEPTEMBER 15, 1951

SPORTS PARADE

By: Curley Grieve
   Sports Editor

Joe Kuharich, an old pro himself, is fiddling with the idea of building an aerial circus at University of San Francisco.

He has the ingredients. But he also has a prejudice against any type of football that isn't based on the fundamental principle of knocking somebody down.

He believes that a player's greatest thrill, transmitted with the speed of light to the spectators in the stands, is a slashing tackle or a crunching block.

"The most savage instinct in man is to assert his physical superiority over somebody else," says Joe. "That's the raw lure of football to the red-blooded kid. He tests his brawn and courage in the fire of combat - and loves it."

Joe is sorry that the trend in football is toward easy touchdowns. The slow march is dead and the quick pass is alive and aerial circuses of the

Southwest left off, have emphasized the futility of bone-cracking attacks when deft overhead shots more easily attain the goal.

It's like the evolution in war making. Military might no longer is expressed entirely in tanks and foot soldiers, gunfire and grenades. The rocket and plane have usurped the throne.

"But these changes, even though dictated by sound strategy, don't necessarily mean we have to sit on the sidelines and applaud," emphasized Kuharich.

"Football's popularity was built upon sheer, primitive physical combat that made spectators shiver. Now it's changed. It's a different game."

"But I still get a greater thrill out of watching George Conner knock Joe Perry on his seat than watching Johnny Lujack complete a pass."

He was referring to the Chicago Bear-San Francisco 49er game. Connor's vicious tackles, especially his collision with Perry, were outstanding features.

Connor, standing like Goliath before the Israelites, was a terrifying spectacle to the customers in the stand.

He was a big part of that football show, no doubt about it.

Kuharich has a Burl Toler, Gino Marchetti, Mike Mergen and Louis Stephens to enact the role of Connor.

But even more pronounced are his weapons to stimulate the Cleveland Browns and Los Angeles Rams, who played for the pro championship last year and again are favored to parlay their passes into a championship playoff this year.

In Ed Brown, the Dons possess an extraordinary passer. Because of his ruggedness, size, finesse, ambition and stick-to-it-iveness, he looms as one of the country's foremost throwers and possibly the No. 1 pick in the professional draft. His All America chances, now that Washington's Don Heinrich is out of the picture, are by no means remote. He could hit the jackpot.

USF has the catchers. Six of them are above average. They are ends Merrill Peacock, Bob St. Clair, Ralph Thomas and Ed Dawson and backs Ollie Matson and Joe Scudero.

Thus Kuharich's threat to concoct an aerial circus has the weight of adequate equipment to support it.

If Kuharich does elect to convert his team into an air force, he will have logic to support his move.

A successful, devastating, spectacular air show would give the Dons distinction and magnetism, box office appeal and national recognition.

It would enhance their chances of landing an important post-season bowl game because it would lift them out of the conventional and spotlight them as different.

It would confer upon the team and new and electric personality that is washable at the gate and in the scheduling of games. Southern Methodist is still riding on the popularity wave it created as an aerial circus - the best national attraction in the Southwest.

One of the troubles with football today is the monotony of the team pattern. There is little to distinguish one team from the other in type of play and strategy. Only the personnel, quantity and quality, and uniforms differ. Even coaching methods are largely standardized.

Coaches dread radical changes because they sometime boomerang. Remember Carl M. Voyles of the Brooklyn club when it belonged to the All America Conference? He conceived the idea of having his linemen stand with hands on knees instead of getting deep down and set for the charge. The maneuver buried him.

Kuharich, holding his present course, can expect a pretty successful season. But he's tempted to shoot for the moon - and pitch forty passes a game instead of twenty.

*   *   *

The Call Bulletin

An Independent Newspaper

VOLUME LXXXIV   MONDAY, SEPTEMBER 17, 1951   10 CENTS

Dink Slaps PCC For Giving USF Runaround
Sked 'Freeze-Out' Back In Force

By: Dink Templeton
     Call Bulletin Special Writer

The more I think about it the greater shame it seems that the USF Dons have been frozen out of even a single Conference game this season, while Santa Clara plays four conference opponents in its first five games.

You'd think old Ed McKeever was still out on the Hilltop, still breathing fire and brimstone at the whole NCAA, while the righteous boys of the ex-Purity Code made certain he'd be boycotted by all the important people.

Ed has been long since gone. The Dons have knuckled in to every hypocritical rule of the PCC. Joe Kuharich has waited and waited at the door for any little handout. How much more do the Dons have to bow and scrape?

Or is it the intention of the Conference fathers to run 'em clean out of business?

Sure, any manager can take you over his schedule and prove to you that he just didn't have any room for Matson, Brown, Scudero, Toler & Co., on his schedule, but that is a lot of applesauce.

A Conference that rules football here in the West, which forces independents to live up to the letter of its own rules which were made especially for their vast organizations of alumni to slink legally by, can scarcely make anyone in his right mind believe that it is just too bad but this is the way it works out, and Santa Clara gets four games and USF none.

Stanford particularly, owes it to USF to get 'em on the schedule and keep 'em there. In the days of the Vow Boys the Spud Lewis teams gave Stanford their best games, only to be dumped off the schedule until the opening day of 1940. The Dons were set for a big season, but finally getting back on the Stanford schedule, plus the fact that the Frankie Albert team was ready to introduce the Shaughnessy T to the Coast, really wrecked the Dons.

So Stanford dumped them again, this time until opening day of 1948. The Dons under Clipper Smith had national publicity, but getting in the big stadium down on the Farm completely over-awed them. What Merriman and the boys did to the over-rated Don finally ran Clipper out of town after a horrible season.

So once again mighty Stanford dumped 'em off the schedule, this time until last year. This playing the big fellow once in a generation makes it pretty tough for the Dons. Once again they went down to the stadium with everyone expecting them to run wild. They didn't have a chance. Marchie's team played the kind of ball it could have played all year - USF froze with stage fright and took a terrible beating, 55 to 7.

But last year's Dons were different. They fought back like wildcats and instead of the beating wrecking their season, it made a fighting outfit of them, one of the best teams to watch the whole season. They won seven and lost four. At the time of the Santa Clara game the Dons were a match for any team on the Coast. The way they played that day they'd have walloped Stanford by plenty, the way Stanford was against Oregon State, Santa Clara, UCLA and Washington, that horrible month before the Cards realized they just weren't putting out.

Frankly, I got more thrill out of the slashing running of little sophomore Joe Scudero than any other back all season. There was no long passer to compare with Ed Brown. Toler may not have been a Pomeroy, quite, backing up the line, but he doubled at tackle on offense, and he wasn't out of the game with injuries as much as Russ.

It was bad enough that the Conference schools grabbed off all the television and killed of the Independent crowds. Now they have to go along with that ridiculous NCAA television rating which brings transcontinental football broadcasts right into San Francisco, while refusing to show USF to televise its games.

I haven't talked this situation over with a single USF man, neither Joe Kuharich or Charley Harney, but they have a right to be boiling mad.

Cal opens with Santa Clara Saturday, and the only reasonable thing would seem to be that Stanford open with USF. They could make it an annual thing, or alternate them.

Instead Stanford goes running all the way to Portland to start the season for the first time away from home, and with Oregon, a Conference team, although fortunately a weak sister, walloped even by little St. Mary's last year, and that seems to be going a long ways out of the way to put a crimp in USF. Certainly the old Freeze Out is back in full force again, with both Cal and Stanford playing all four of the schools of Northern Division, of which only Washington means anything at all in these parts.

I do not think either Brutus Hamilton or Al Masters wants to force any more colleges clear out of football. St. Mary's and Nevada in one year was a pretty bad jolt. I can't believe that the story of the Don center throwing a punch in the Stanford game could call for a boycott. Nor that Cal would actually be insulted because Kuharich said the Dons would have walloped the Bears on a dry field - which they might just have done at that. But if they had anything more than that against USF it's about time they come out with it openly. For though they might legitimately have been unable to find room for San Francisco, it's a little strange that all the other conference colleges found themselves in the same fix.

At the end of the season, the little Dons were the fastest starting and hardest charging team in these parts, a pretty darn gallant little bunch, and unless they're stealing the silver out of someone's training table, they do not deserve the boycott treatment.

*   *   *

7 GRANITE BLOCKS | CALL BULLETIN SPORTS
THURSDAY, SEPTEMBER 6, 1951 Page 17

Weibel, St. Clair, Mergen, Toler, Tringali, Marchetti, and Thomas

The Call Bulletin

An Independent Newspaper

VOLUME LXXXIV   MONDAY, SEPTEMBER 17, 1951   10 CENTS

Daley Says: USF Team Best In History

By: Walt Daley

No matter how the football bounces, nor no matter how much aqua flows beneath the bridge between now and December, the University of San Francisco gridders today loom on papyrus as kings of the coast independents for the 1951 football season.

You could never get Coach Joe Kuharich to make that statement, but, nevertheless, you can't get around it.

Kuharich will sit down with you and blow smoke for hours on the talents of nearly every one of his 52 Don squad members, but put them all together as one big powerhouse machine and point it out to the ex-Notre Damer, and he crawls into a shell.

"We haven't got enough guns," he says, " We do not go deep enough."

Not enough guns? Not deep enough? How many guns does it take to pop a target right on the bullseye? In this respect, of course, Kuharich is no different than any other coach. Give them enough big, experienced and clever men to place in a hole in the earth from here "down to China," as the kids in the back yard say, and they'll still tell you "we don't go deep enough."

The USF schedule for 1951 is obviously weaker than it was in 1950, through no fault of the Dons themselves who were trying as late as two weeks ago to bolster it - and the team is stronger. One ace is gone from the backfield (Roy Barni) and one ace is gone from the line (Dick Stanfel) and to offset the loss is the fact that several bright new prospects grace the roster and each and every one of the veterans are one year older, a little more experienced.

The one fellow on the Hilltop who has every right to be frantic is Publicity Man, Pete Rozelle. He'll be lucky if he's able to start the ball rolling for even one USF candidate for All American and he's got at least four such prospects on his hands. If he's all out for Fullback Ollie Matson, what of Quarterback Ed Brown, Linebacker Toler, or Tackle Gino Marchetti?

Fortunately for the Don football coaching staff, which might prefer to have the drums beat with a trifle softer tone, it must be pointed out that the Dons did lose last year to two teams that are also on this year's schedule - Fordham and Loyola.

They should not have lost either of those two contests, however, admittedly "blowing the duke" in final moments of play, Fordham followers frankly complimented the Dons as the strongest eleven they had played that year.

All of this adds up to a campaign now for an undefeated season. USF has never had one and it is the biggest incentive the grid kids on the Hilltop can muster up since they have neither California nor Stanford games to look forward to this year.

Line Coach Bud Kerr has under his wing a better defensive forward wall than ever before on the Hilltop. Save for Stanfel's loss it is the same, to the man, as the group which in 1950 allowed a total of only 820 yards rushing against it in 11 games. That was an average of 74.5 per game and enabled USF to finish fourth among the nation's collegiate elevens in rushing defense. The leader was Ohio State, allowing but 64 yards average per tilt.

Across the line to dig in and hold 'em, Kerr will have Ralph Thomas, Gino Marchetti, Vince Tringali, Lou Stephens, Bob St. Clair and Bob Weibel. Backing up the line are Roy Giorgi and Burl Toler. Top-weighters among this group are Marchetti at 225, Stephens at 225 and St. Clair at 235.

Turn now to the touchdown department, the men who make with the six-pointers better than any Dons before them have done. The 200-pound Matson packs the mail again from the fullback post. He's the guy who slowed up a little in his junior year yet managed to build up his touchdown total to

20 in two seasons. He was the leading scorer in the West with thirteen touchdowns and three conversions for 81 points.

DONS '50 RECORD

USF	OPPONENT	
23	Tulsa	14
7	Stanford	55
66	Nevada	6
33	St. Mary's	7
27	San Jose State	0
14	Fordham	21
24	Denver	6
27	Santa Clara	6
7	California	13
35	Detroit	13
28	Loyola	40
291		181

Won 7, Lost 4

Matson's longest runs were 63 yards against Tulsa, 64 against Denver and 41 against Fordham on a pass play. He galloped to a 37-yard runback to a touchdown with a pass interception against Denver. All performances except the Tulsa one were in spite of a hamstring muscle injury. He equals any member of the squad, too, as a defensive player.

Quarterback Ed Brown is a picture of perfection as an aerial artist. He set new school records for: (1) The most passes ever thrown in one season, 140; (2) the most completions in one season, 59; (3) the most yards ever gained by passes in one season, 1,205; and (4) the most touchdown passes thrown, 10.

Brown rifled two of the longest passes these eyes have ever seen on consecutive downs in the Fordham game as victory flew out the window in the final seconds. Both traveled 60 yards in the air and both were completed. The first was called back and the Dons penalized for offsides. The second netted 80 yards in all as Merrill Peacock rambled 20 after the catch.

Besides, the converted backfielder Peacock, Brown has excellent pass receivers to throw to in Ends Thomas, St. Clair, Dawson and Bob Weibel. Assuming the Dons will stick to their diversified T-formation attack, several of the ball-toting backfield stars can plan on gathering Brown's strato-tosses as well.

Not to be overlooked in the Don offensive is little Joe ("Scooter") Scudero, a sensation as a sophomore, who won himself a starting berth at left half in no time at all. He crossed the final white stripe for touchdown no less than nine times in 1950 and climaxed a spectacular season for such a little guy with a 62 yard, broken field romp with a punt to a touchdown against Loyola.

And should Quarterback Bill Henneberry (Brown's replacement), and Backs George Carley, Vince Sakowski, Jim Boggan and Dick Huxley show as much improvement as they did in the season past, the Dons indeed have backfield aces to spare. In the line Harold Sachs and Greg Hillig step up for mention, assuring the Dons should be deep enough not only for the San Jose Staters in the opener September 21, but the others to follow.

U.S.F. SCHEDULE FOR 1951

September 21	San Jose State at Kezar (night)
September 29	Idaho at Boise
October 7	Camp Pendleton Marines at Kezar
October 12	San Jose State at San Jose (night)
October 20	Fordham at New York
October 26	San Diego Naval Training Center at Kezar (night)
November 4	Santa Clara at Kezar
November 17	College of the Pacific at Stockton (night)
November 25	Loyola of Los Angeles at Pasadena

*   *   *

The actors in place, the stage was now set. The University of San Francisco Dons were getting ready to kick off their '51 season—straight into collegiate football history.

CHAPTER SIX
Kick Off To Glory

"We knew we could beat any team in the country."

—Quarterback Ed Brown - 1951

Kicking off the `51 season

San Francisco Examiner

Monarch of the Dailies

FRIDAY, SEPTEMBER 21, 1951

USF Choice Over San Jose Tonight
Matson, Brown & Co. Flash Under Lights at Kezar

By: Curley Grieve
    Sports Editor

The University of San Francisco launches its "year of decision" in football tonight when it faces San Jose State College under Kezar's crown of lights.

The Dons, blessed with a team that could stamp itself best in Hilltop history, are fighting for life.

Theirs is a case of discouragement. At the peak of a cycle, with a matured and able squad, they were frozen off Pacific Coast Conference schedules.

Thus, with honors and trumps in abundance, they didn't get an opportunity to play the hand in a fast league.

It was a blow to their pride, hopes and budget. In despair there was a whisper:

"This is the beginning of the end of football at USF."

But the Dons—players and alumni, faculty and followers—have rebounded with greater determination, fashioned a post-season bowl game objective, and announced an ambition to **"get under the skin and into the heart"** of the city.

*   *   *

USF Fans at Kezar Stadium and "The Trumpet's Charge"

USF's 1951 GRIDIRON TEAM ROSTER

NAME	POS	AGE	WT.	HT.	CLASS	EXP.	HOMETOWN
Arnoldy, Dick	E	17	175	6.1	FR	HS	Marysville
Becker, Jack	G	18	185	6	FR	HS	Pittsburg, Calif.
Boggan, Jim	HB	20	185	6	JR	1V	Willows
Brown, Ed	QB	22	212	6.2	SR	2V	San Luis Obispo
Bruna, Roy	C	19	205	5.11	SO	FR.	San Francisco
Carley, George	HB	23	187	5.11	SR	2V	Eureka
Chess, Gene	HB	19	163	5.8	SO	FR.	Chicago
Colombini, Dick	G	19	200	5.11	JR	1V	Santa Rosa
Cronan, John	QB	18	192	6.2	SO	FR.	San Francisco
Dando, Bill	HB	18	185	6	SO	FR.	Gordon, Pa.
Dawson, Ed	E	21	193	6.1	SR	2V	Santa Monica
DeBernardi, Jim	G	18	180	5.11	SO	FR.	San Francisco
Dwyer, John	G	18	185	5.1	SO	FR.	Chicago

NAME	POS	AGE	WT.	HT.	CLASS	EXP.	HOMETOWN
Giorgi, Roy	FB	23	195	5.11	SR	2V	San Francisco
Henneberry, Bill	QB	20	180	5.11	SR	2V	San Francisco
Hillig, Greg	C	20	185	5.11	SR	2V	Cochrane, Wis.
Holm, John	E	18	205	6.3	FR	HS	San Francisco
Huxley, Dick	FB	20	188	5.11	JR	1V	San Francisco
Kearney, Jim	HB	20	175	5.11	JR	1V	San Francisco
Madden, Leo	G	18	195	5.1	SO	FR.	Omaha, Neb.
Marchetti, Gino	T	25	225	6.3	SR	2V	Antioch
Matson, Ollie	FB	21	203	6.2	SR	2V	San Francisco
McLaughlin, Frank	E	20	190	5.11	JR	1V	Chicago
McMahon, Larry	T	18	205	6	FR	HS	Chicago
Mergen, Mike	T	23	248	6.5	SR	2V	McHenry, Ill.
Montero, Tom	E	19	190	6	SO	FR.	Loomis
Monti, Frank	E	19	210	6.1	SO	FR.	Minersville, Pa.
Moriarity, Tim	T	18	220	5.1	SO	FR.	Chicago
Peacock, Merrill	E	24	185	6	SR	2V	San Francisco
Retzloff, Jack	HB	21	187	6	JR	1JC	Eureka
Roland, Walter	QB	19	167	6	SO	FR.	Shenandoah, Pa.
Sachs, Harold	C	20	200	6.2	SR	1V	Pasadena
Sakowski, Vince	HB	23	170	5.9	SR	2V	Shenandoah, Pa.
Scudero, Joe	HB	21	165	5.1	JR	1V	San Francisco
Schaeffer, Bob	G	20	187	5.9	SO	FR.	Chicago
Skalla, Bill	C	17	165	5.1	FR	HS	Omaha, Neb.
Slajchert, Larry	C	18	214	6.1	SO	FR.	Chicago
Springer, Bob	HB	18	165	5.1	SO	FR.	San Francisco
St. Clair, Bob	E	20	235	6.7	JR.	1V	San Francisco
Stephens, Louis	G	20	225	6	SR	2V	Oakland
Thiel, John	HB	19	190	5.11	SO	FR.	Chicago
Thomas, Ralph	E	21	193	5.11	SR	2V	Racine, Wis.
Toler, Burl	C	22	210	6.2	SR	2V	Oakland
Tringali, Vince	G	22	205	6	SR	1V	San Francisco
Weibel, Bob	E	22	190	6	SR	2V	Allentown, Pa.
Welsh, Harmon	T	18	218	5.11	SO	FR.	Port Chicago, Calif.
Whitney, Jim	HB	19	180	5.1	SO	FR.	Burlingame
Wilwerding, Bob	G	18	180	5.11	FR	HS	Omaha, Neb.

USF Offensive

LE	LT	LG	C	RG	RT	RE
Peacock	Marchetti	Hillig	Sachs	Stephens	Toler	St.Clair
McLaughlin	Moriarity	Dwyer	Slajchert	Conte	Mergen	Thomas
Dawson	Tringali	Madden	Bruno	De Bernardi	Welsh	Weibel

QB

Brown

Henneberry

Hauser

LH	FB	RH
Scudero	Matson	Carley
Boggan	Huxley	Sakowski
Chess	Whitney	Thiel

USF Defensive

LE	LT	LG	RG	RT	RE
Thomas	Marchetti	Tringali	Stephens	St. Clair	Weibel
McLaughlin	Moriarity	Hillig	De Bernardi	Mergen	St. Clair
Peacock	Tringali	Mergen	Shaeffer	Welsh	Holm

LEFT LINEBACKER	RIGHT LINEBACKER
Giorgi	Toler
Madden	Henneberry
Colombini	Carley

LH	SAFETY	RH
Matson	Scudero	Brown
Peacock	Kearney	Carley
Thiel	Arenivar	Kearney

GAME 1: USF 39, SAN JOSE STATE 2

(September 21, 1951)

San Jose State dropped under a 39-2 pounding by the entire USF team. The backs, tackles, guards, centers, and ends all played an integral part in this win. Ollie Matson, in top form against the Spartans, raced up and down the field for 127 yards and two touchdowns. Ed Brown shelled San Jose with completions to ends Merrill Peacock and Bob St. Clair. Before the evening was over, Peacock had scored three touchdowns while St. Clair crossed the goal line for another six points. The versatile Brown also kicked three times, wrapping up all three conversions. In the course of the action, he completed 19 out of 34 passes for 261 yards.

The defense also did its part. Burl Toler, Gino Marchetti, Mike Mergen and St. Clair, allowed the Spartans only 61 yards on the ground. Even more astounding was the fact that San Jose State had not completed a first down until the remaining twelve minutes of the game! By that time, it was all but over and the Dons had walked away with their first win of the season.

Dons record: 1-0-0

USF		SJS
19	1ST DOWNS	4
161	NET RUSHING YDS	61
263	NET PASSING YDS	54
34	PASSES ATTEMPTED	17
19	PASSES COMPLETED	7
4	INTERCEPTIONS	2
37.3	PUNTING AVG	21
40	PUNT RETURN YDS	27
36	KICKOFF RETURN YDS	128

Scudero scoots for gain

GAME 2: USF 28, IDAHO 7

(September 29, 1951)

The Dons traveled to Boise where they changed from a fierce aerial attacking force to a deadly running team in the course of a week. This was definitely Matson's day to shine as he ran for 235 yards in 33 carries and added three more touchdowns to his career. Ollie scored his final td early in the fourth quarter on a 68 yard sprint that bolted through the right side of the Idaho line. The defense, led by Marchetti, Toler and St. Clair, once again turned in a strong performance.

The fourth touchdown of the day was carried out on a mid-field punt return by Joe Scudero. Ed Brown threw a key block that allowed Scudero to score, but wrenched a back muscle in the process. Bill Henneberry took over as quarterback, and led the Hilltoppers to the win.

Dons record: 2-0-0

USF		IDAHO
21	1ST DOWNS	9
251	NET RUSHING YDS	95
147	NET PASSING YDS	147
21	PASSES ATTEMPTED	27
10	PASSES COMPLETED	10
2	INTERCEPTIONS	2
47	PUNTING AVG	45
n/a	PUNT RETURN YDS	n/a
n/a	KICKOFF RETURN YDS	n/a

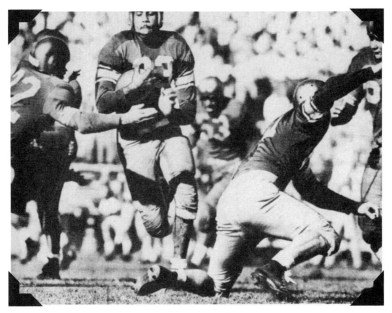

Matson comes through a gap.

Defensive men, Brown (15), Thomas (87), Toler (55), Whitney (38), smear El Bronco.

GAME 3: USF 26, CAMP PENDLETON MARINES 0
(October 7, 1951)

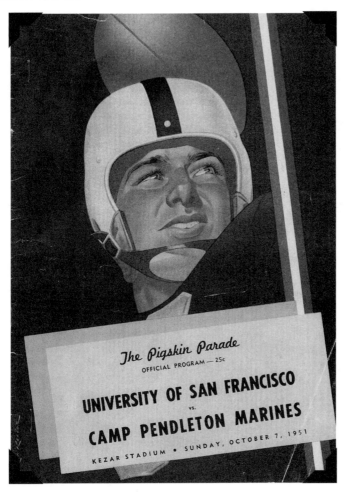

The Dons played host to the Camp Pendleton Marines at Kezar Stadium. The Leathernecks' team roster included a balanced mixture of former pro football personnel, former college football players, and an All Pro end. Included in this talented squad were: Walt Szot, ex Chicago Cardinal and Pittsburgh Steeler tackle; Bob Burl, ex Chicago Bear tackle; Cloyce Box, 1950 All Pro with the Detroit Lions; Gene Valentine, ex Rice University guard; Charlie Harris, University of Georgia back; and Joe Cribari, honorable mention All American center from Denver University. This impressive lineup, however, did not impress the Dons. And quarterback Bill Henneberry captured his first full Varsity game victory while Ed Brown received treatments for a back injury.

A brilliant combination of offensive calls by Henneberry and defensive calls by Burl Toler produced a 26-0 win for USF. The Marines ended up with a minus 47 yards rushing. Matson picked up two touchdowns and Roy Giorgi intercepted a Cloyce Box pass and ran it back for six points. Mc Laughlin sealed the Marines' fate with a pass that resulted in an 80 yard td.

Dons record: 3-0-0

USF		PENDLETON
8	1ST DOWNS	4
212	NET RUSHING YDS	37
59	NET PASSING YDS	35
9	PASSES ATTEMPTED	23
2	PASSES COMPLETED	4
5	INTERCEPTIONS	3
41.3	PUNTING AVG	40.8
49	PUNT RETURN YDS	87
0	KICKOFF RETURN YDS	91

Scudero scoots to score

A pitch out from Henneberry to Matson who smashes a marine

GAME 4: USF 42, SAN JOSE STATE 7

(October 12, 1951)

After blowing the Spartans out of their own stadium by a score of 39-2 three weeks ago, the Dons, for a second time, faced San Jose. Although the Spartans tried desperately to save face, it was once again, in vane. Matson scored three times while Scudero, Dick Huxley and Vince Sakowski contributed with one touchdown each. Burl Toler capitalized on a San Jose miscue for a safety. Four conversions were provided by center Hal Sachs, which gave the Dons a total of 42 points. A pass play and conversion gave the Spartans their only touchdown.

Dons record: 4-0-0

USF		SJS
21	1ST DOWNS	3
369	NET RUSHING YDS	88
5	NET PASSING YDS	162
10	PASSES ATTEMPTED	27
1	PASSES COMPLETED	12
1	INTERCEPTIONS	2
	32.3 PUNTING AVG	35.5
31	PUNT RETURN YDS	20
40	KICKOFF RETURN YDS	116

Offense in action

FORDHAM (PRE GAME)

The Dons' Athletic News Director, Pete Rozelle, flew back to New York one week ahead of the team to try to convince New York sportswriters that Matson and the rest of the USF team were more than just another football team. They were something very 'special'. Before leaving, he talked to Matson. "Ollie," Rozelle said, "if you don't do well in New York, you can forget about being an All American. Now is the time to show people back there we've got some football players out here."

Upon arriving in New York, Rozelle contacted Grantland Rice who was the writer of a widely syndicated newspaper column. Rice was also known for his Grantland Rice's, All American Picks for *Look Magazine*. Pete pulled out all the stops with the seventh-one year old Rice. He even took the time to pick him up and drive him to the game himself!

GAME 5: USF 32, FORDHAM 26

(October 20, 1951)

Making believers of the New York sportswriters, Ollie Matson made good his claim for All American honors by returning not one, but two kickoff returns for touchdowns; the first was for 94 yards and the second for 90 yards. Fordham players could not stop him despite the fact that he fumbled the kickoff both times before picking up the ball and leaving the entire Rams' squad in the dust. Ollie scored yet another touchdown late in the third period giving him a total of three for the day.

Fordham tried to run through USF's defense but was immediately cut down by Toler, Marchetti, Hillig, Thomas, St. Clair, and Sachs. When the offense was changed to the pass, the Rams' end, Tom Healy, was consistently attacked and pulled down by Marchetti and St. Clair. However, Fordham did manage to score 26 points, but with 74 seconds left to go in the game, quarterback Ed Brown rushed for three yards and crossed the goal line to capture the win. The Dons win their fifth straight game.

Afterward, Ed Danowski, Fordham's coach, was quoted as saying, "I can't see how they can keep Matson off anyone's All America" (Bucky Walter, sportswriter, S.F. Examiner, October 51).

The following day, Harold Rosenthal of the *New York Herald Tribune* wrote, "Rozelle should have 'his stripes removed' for not telling the members of the fourth estate 'more' about this extraordinary runner (Matson)."

After this game USF ranked 20th in the Associated Press top 20 poll.

Dons record: 5-0-0

USF		FORDHAM
14	1ST DOWNS	8
216	NET RUSHING YDS	61
89	NET PASSING YDS	253
14	PASSES ATTEMPTED	31
5	PASSES COMPLETED	16
1	INTERCEPTIONS	1
35	PUNTING AVG	49.5
30	PUNT RETURN YDS	24
n/a	KICKOFF RETURN YDS	n/a

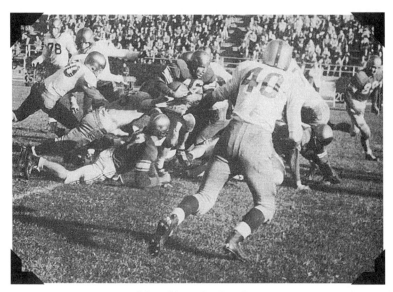

Sakowski smashes Ram line

Sakowski smashes Ram line

Associated Press

TUESDAY, OCTOBER 23, 1951

Ollie One Of Best—Kuharich

By: Will Grimsley, New York

It's too bad fullback Ollie Matson isn't on a big time football team, says San Francisco's football coach, Joe Kuharich. "He'd be rated one of the greatest players of all times."

If Ollie were with California, or Notre Dame or Michigan, he'd be hailed as another Jim Thorpe or Red Grange." the young coach of the Jesuit Dons declared today.

"He has speed, strength and power such as I've never seen before. He can do anything and do it almost to perfection. He's a great runner as you know. He can also block, tackle, receive and hawk passes."

"I have seen all the great backs since 1926 when I was a kid - Marchy Schwartz, Joe Savoldi, Marty Brill, Marshall Goldberg and Bill Dudley."

"Some of them might have been able to do one thing better than Ollie. None could do everything as well."

Kuharich, whose Dons defeated Fordham Saturday at the Polo grounds 32-26, spared no adjectives in describing his senior fullback star.

"Furthermore, the San Francisco coach added, "I don't think Matson has reached his full potential. He's still young (21) as football players go and he's only been playing a few years. He should make a tremendous pro player."

*   *   *

Eastern writers hardly needed a speech to sell them on this six foot two, 203 pound San Franciscan. They saw Matson run back two kickoffs 94 and 90 yards for touchdowns.

★ ★ ★ HALFTIME ★ ★ ★

USF Halftime activities at Kezar Stadium

Dons gear up for second half of `51 season

GAME 6:
USF 26, SAN DIEGO NAVAL TRAINING CENTER 7

(October 26, 1951)

The Dons returned home to Kezar Stadium to face the San Diego Naval Training Center. The Bluejackets were the surprise victors earlier this season over Loyola. Not unlike the Camp Pendleton Marines, San Diego carried a roster compiled of former professional and former collegiate stars. Names like running back, Odie Posey from the Los Angeles Rams; George Musacco, fullback on Loyola's 1950 championship team, Ken Jackson, 240 pound All Southwest Conference tackle from the University of Texas; Bucky Curtis, All American from Vanderbilt University, quarterback Don Logue from the University of Arkansas and Ralph Cochran from the University of Alabama.

The Bluejackets took control early in the first quarter, but then USF erupted. Matson rushed from the Dons 45 yard line to the Navy 17. Minutes later, Brown connected with St. Clair on a 17 yard pass for the Hilltopper's first score. Brown fired a 24 yard pass to Peacock to gave USF a 13-0 lead. From that point on, it was USF all the way. Matson scored in the closing minutes of the second quarter, but the td was called back due to a penalty. Matson again scored in the third quarter on a 28 yard run, his fourteenth of the season. Score: 20-0. In the fourth, Brown bootlegged from the two and USF now lead 26-0. With eleven minutes left to play in the game, Ralph Cochran threw for 24 yards to Gallie McCormack for the Navy's only score of the day. At the conclusion of this game, USF was still ranked 20th in the AP top 20 poll.

Dons record: 6-0-0

USF		SAN DIEGO NAVY
18	1ST DOWNS	9
374	NET RUSHING YDS	71
94	NET PASSING YDS	131
17	PASSES ATTEMPTED	31
8	PASSES COMPLETED	15
1	INTERCEPTIONS	3
38.8	PUNTING AVG	39.2
27	PUNT RETURN YDS	20
25	KICKOFF RETURN YDS	138

Don Fullback piledrives to score

"All the way Ollie"

GAME 7: USF 26, SANTA CLARA 7

(November 4, 1951)

Walt Daley, sportswriter for the San Francisco Call-Bulletin, had this to say before the start of the USF-Santa Clara game.

"Even though they were picked to be a 13 point favorite over Santa Clara, Coach Kuharich was still a little apprehensive about the predicted win. "We've only beaten Santa Clara once in twelve years," Kuharich screams as his open salvo, "They're always tough and I'm betting they'll be twice as tough this year with the incentive for knocking off an undefeated team."

It was a balmy Sunday afternoon in Kezar Stadium where 32,685 fans eagerly awaited the twenty-second meeting of the USF-Santa Clara traditional gridiron clash. The USF/Santa Clara series record is: Santa Clara 17 wins, USF 3 wins and 1 tie. This would be the Hilltoppers final collegiate home appearance. The stage was now set for this "classic" rivalry to begin.

The Dons led 7-0 at the half with Matson racking up 56 of the 66 yards gained before capping off the march with his two yard run across the goal line. In the opening minutes of the second half, SC quarterback, Johnny Pasco, turned a short screen pass into a 64 yard scoring play. But the Bronc's elation was cut short when George Carley intercepted a Pasco pass and crossed the goal line for 6. Before the final gun sounded ending the game, Matson scored twice, giving him a total of seventeen touchdowns in seven games; a total of 102 points; .the best record in the country.

The 26-7 suppression of Santa Clara's Broncos represented the Dons' seventh straight win of the season, something they had never done before. After this game, USF was ranked 15th in the AP top 20 poll.

Dons record: 7-0-0

USF		SANTA CLARA
10	1ST DOWNS	3
321	NET RUSHING YDS	-18
58	NET PASSING YDS	235
15	PASSES ATTEMPTED	35
6	PASSES COMPLETED	19
2	INTERCEPTIONS	2
43.7	PUNTING AVG	40.1
86	PUNT RETURN YDS	74
19	KICKOFF RETURN YDS	78

Don offense opens a hole for ace fullback

Bob St. Clair snags a pass

COLLEGE OF PACIFIC - PRE GAME
San Francisco Chronicle
The City's Only Home-Owned Newspaper

FOUNDED 1865   SAN FRANCISCO. SATURDAY, NOVEMBER 17, 1951   GA 1-1112

Unbeaten Dons Face Pacific
By: Dick Friendlich

Six months ago, when the revised football schedules for Bay Area football teams were completed, the experts predicted that the winner of the USF-College of the Pacific football game on November 17 would be in line for a post-season bowl game bid.

Well, here it is, November 17, and the Dons and the Tigers will be going at it tonight before an expected overflow crowd of 40,000 in Stockton's Memorial Stadium, and there may be a bowl bid for the winner - if the winner is USF.

Considering what usually happens to such long range predictions, this one has stood up very well. Coach Joe Kuharich's Dons come into the battle undefeated and untied in seven games, with the best defensive record against rushing in the country, with an All American fullback candidate in Ollie Matson, the country's rushing leader. The Tigers, coached by Ernie Jorge, playing a schedule considerably tougher than the Dons slate, have won six out of eight, their victims including a very good Clemson eleven which may pick off a bowl bid itself. South Carolina has been the only team besides COP to beat Clemson.

Macon and Putnam

The Tigers have their own All American candidates in Eddie Macon, a swift halfback, and Duane Putnam, a fine linebacker and a wicked lead blocker on the COP sweep. But upset defeats at the hands of Boston University and Denver have cost the Tigers their own chances for a bowl. There remains for them only the satisfaction of splattering the Dons' unbeaten record.

Although Coach Kuharich has repeatedly declared he does not think his team will get a bowl invitation there is a die hard group on the Hilltop which believes that a decisive victory tonight will get the Dons an invitation.

Three weeks ago Orange Bowl officials included USF among eleven teams "under consideration" for the game. Subsequently, the Orange Bowlers chose Georgia Tech as one half of the New Year's Day game, but except for the Rose Bowl, and Sugar Bowl, other post season berths (four, roughly) remain unfilled.

The Dons have been established 7 to 10 point favorites. They have a well-balanced team - big, fast linemen led by Gino Marchetti at tackle and Burl Toler at linebacker, a great passer in Ed Brown, and strong running support for Matson in wiry Joe Scudero. If they have a weakness, it is lack of depth. Matson, Brown, Scudero, Bob St. Clair and George Carley are among those counted upon to go both ways.

No Passes...But

COP has one of the strongest running games in the country, going against a line that has not yielded a touchdown this year. The Tigers' Macon, Tom McCormick, Al Smith and Art Liebscher have averaged 344 yards per game on the ground, In fact the Tigers have run so well all season that their quarterbacks have shown complete disdain for the forward pass, even when its use would seem the wise move.

This tendency to view use of the pass as a confession of weakness should be buried tonight. Jorge has named Doug Scovil as the starting quarterback ahead of Tony Geremia, a superior ball-handler but not as good a passer as Scovil. The tiger coach has said several times before: "We're going to pass this Saturday."

This time he means it.

*   *   *

GAME 8: USF 47, COLLEGE OF THE PACIFIC 14

(November 17, 1951)

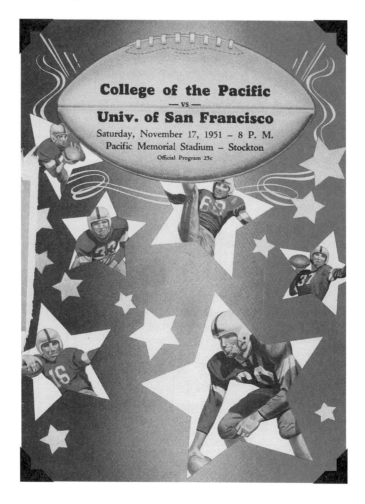

John Peri, Stockton Record sports editor, wrote, "Going into this game, San Francisco was eighth in total offense in the nation, ninth in rushing, third in total defense and first in rushing defense. Pacific was sixth in total offense, third in rushing and tenth in rushing defense."

A crowd of 41,607 filled the Bengals' Pacific Memorial Stadium as the College of Pacific once again fell victim to the University of San Francisco's undefeated and untied Dons, 47-14. USF scored three times in the first twenty minutes of the game. Early in the first quarter, halfbacks Tom

McCormick and Eddie Macon committed errors by fielding punts that should have been allowed to bounce into the end zone for touchbacks. McCormick bobbled a punt return that resulted in Marchetti recovering for USF. One play later, Matson ran it in for the score. Macon fielded the second goal line punt late in the opening period but was stopped at the four. On the second play he lost control of the ball allowing Ralph Thomas to recover for the Dons. A few plays later, quarterback Ed Brown lobbed a pass to end Bob St. Clair for the second score of the game - USF 14, COP 0.

In the second quarter, Macon fumbled again; this time recovered by St. Clair. A missed blocking assignment in the COP backfield allowed Burl Toler to block a punt in the end zone where guard Mike Mergen collapsed on it to take a 20-0 lead at the half.

Held to 31 net yards in the first half, the Tigers came out roaring and dominated the entire third quarter. A fumble by Matson enabled COP to move the ball 20 yards down field in ten plays. Halfback Hank Welch dove over the goal line from two yards out making the score 20-7. Just as Pacific began to get its hopes up, Matson sprinted for a 68 yard touchdown early in the fourth quarter, his nineteenth of the season. From that point on it was as if the Tigers had given up. Ed Brown would throw for three more touchdowns before the game was over. First, Brown caught Merrill Peacock in the end zone with a 24 yard pass. The second score began with a fake to Matson, then hitting St. Clair for a 35 yard td. With seconds left in the game and no open receivers, Brown rushed for 31 yards for the final USF touchdown, giving the Dons their largest point total of the year, 47. Prior to Brown's run, Pacific's Doug Scovil connected with Macon for a 21 yard score. But as the saying goes, 'It was too little, too late.' Matson outgained Macon, 178 yards to 80. In the end, COP could hardly expect to win after giving up the ball nine times - five on fumbles and four on pass interceptions. USF won 47-14. The Dons remain undefeated. They had hopes of a post season invitation to either the Orange, Cotton, or Gator Bowl, but as yet, no overtures had reached the Hilltop.

USF was ranked 13th in the AP top 20 poll.

Dons record: 8-0-0

USF		COP
7	1ST DOWNS	18
253	NET RUSHING YDS	168
97	NET PASSING YDS	200
17	PASSES ATTEMPTED	32
7	PASSES COMPLETED	15
4	INTERCEPTIONS	3
41.9	PUNTING AVG	21.4
0	PUNT RETURN YDS	0
0	KICKOFF RETURN YDS	0

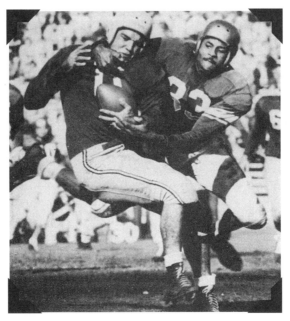

Don defense breaks El Bronco

Passer, Ed Brown, carries the ball for a touchdown

LOYOLA - PRE GAME
The Call Bulletin

VOLUME LXXXIV   NOVEMBER, 1951   10 CENTS

Orange Bowl People Say—
Dons' Bowl Bid Chances Bettered

By: Walt Daley
    Sportswriter

Though there has been no jingle on the telephone for a bowl invitation as yet, and none likely until next week, the undefeated University of San Francisco gridders nevertheless had added incentive today for their Loyola game in Pasadena next Sunday.

Not only have the Dons their first undefeated season within grasp, but word from the Orange Bowl people yesterday assured them an even better chance of landing the Orange Bowl "plum" than most people suspected.

Both the Orange Bowl's committee chairman, Van C. Kussrow, and another selection committee member, have been quoted as "favoring a California representation." The Dons, if lucky enough to win the bid, can thank their Santa Clara neighbors for the fine impression the Broncs made in walloping Kentucky in the Miami New Year's Day classic of 1950.

Hold Up Vote

The Orange Bowl people voted, however, to hold up on picking an opponent for Georgia Tech, already one of the teams selected until the Southwest Conference race becomes a little clearer, Baylor, Texas, Rice and Texas Christian are also being considered by the Orange Bowl, as is Oklahoma.

USF's injured members, in the meantime, were reported "resting" and coming along fine. Joe Scudero's heel injury won't keep him out of the lineup against Loyola. Gino Marchetti's ankle contains no broken bone as first feared, and he should be ready, and Ollie Matson's injured rib shows no crack. He'll be able to go against the Loyolans, too.

There is much to gain on both sides when the Lions and Dons collide in Pasadena Sunday afternoon. A good day, or even a mediocre one, will see Don Klosterman set a new collegiate passing record. Ollie Matson can better the rushing record for one season by gaining 118 yards on the ground —and can top the all time scoring mark if he manages to hit pay dirt on three occasions.

Matson Honored

Yesterday afternoon, Matson was named All-this and All-that and All-what have you as Northern California grid writers met at their weekly luncheon He was named Northern California's outstanding back of the year. The grid writers also wired the Orange Bowl committee recommending that the Dons be awarded a bid.

*   *   *

GAME 9: USF 20, LOYOLA 2

(November 25, 1951)

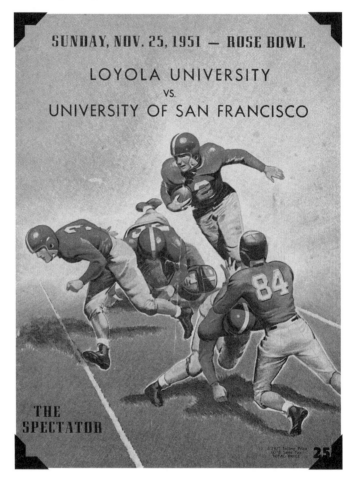

USF kept its bowl chances alive with a convincing 20-2 victory over a surprisingly strong Loyola defense. Nearly 16,000 spectators at the Rose Bowl witnessed USF's ninth straight triumph and the first perfect season in the history of the University.

The battle between the nation's leading rusher, Ollie Matson of USF, and the nation's top passer, Don Klosterman of Loyola, turned out to be just that. Lions' coach Jordan Olivers stacked an eight man line that followed Matson's every move. The Dons were also without the support of All Coast tackle, Gino Marchetti, who was out with a foot injury.

When the smoke of battle had cleared, it was learned that Matson's 112 yard total fell four yards short of surpassing the all time collegiate mark of 1570; his two touchdowns scored against Loyola gave him a season total of twenty-one, one short of the national season mark of twenty-two held jointly by Bobby Reynolds (Nebraska), and Whizzer White (Arizona State).

Even though Klosterman completed 51 per cent of his passes by connecting on twenty-four of forty-seven attempts, the Lions were still unable to cross the Dons' goal line. USF's defensive line limited Loyola runners to a mere 44 yards, less than half a football field!

The score was still 0-0 at the end of the first quarter. In the second quarter, USF scored first with a 6 yard run by Matson. Loyola's only score of the day was a safety made by tackle Ernie Cheatham, who blocked an attempted punt by Brown. The ball rebounded into the end zone where Brown picked it up and was tagged by Cheatham for the 2 points.

The longest run of the day was made by Dick Huxley, Matson's backup. While Ollie was catching his breath, Huxley broke through the middle and ran for 72 yards to the Lion 8. Two plays later, Brown hit end Ralph Thomas on the 6 for the second Dons' touchdown.

USF's final score came during the third quarter when Matson bolted over the goal line from the 1. Linebacker Burl Toler had intercepted Klosterman on the Lion 31. The Dons moved the ball down field to the 1 yard line where Ollie made his move; thus closing the book forever on his incredible collegiate football career. After this game, USF was ranked 14th in the AP top 20.

Dons record: 9-0-0

USF		LOYOLA
15	1ST DOWNS	17
259	NET RUSHING YDS	44
49	NET PASSING YDS	211
12	PASSES ATTEMPTED	47
3	PASSES COMPLETED	24
4	INTERCEPTIONS	0
33	PUNTING AVG	45
n/a	PUNT RETURN YDS	n/a
n/a	KICKOFF RETURN YDS	n/a

A Don outflanks Lions

McLaughlin (81), Scudero (13), Mergen (77),
lay key blocks for Don touchdown

UNIVERSITY OF SAN FRANCISCO
FINAL STATS FOR NINE GAMES

USF		OPPONENTS
2769	TOTAL YARDS - RUSHING	884
225	TOTAL YARDS LOST - RUSHING	410
2544	NET YARDS GAINED - RUSHING	474
153	FORWARD PASSES ATTEMPTED	273
60	FORWARD PASSES COMPLETED	122
880	NET YARDS GAINED - PASSING	1421
12	PASSES RESULTING IN TD'S	9
23	PASSES INTERCEPTED BY	18
236	YRDS. RETURNED - INTERCEPTED PASSES	258
667	NUMBER OF OFFENSIVE PLAYS	561
3430	NET GAIN IN TOTAL OFFENSE	1895
101	FIRST DOWNS - RUSHING	35
28	FIRST DOWNS - PASSING	50
7	FIRST DOWNS - PENALTIES	5
136	TOTAL FIRST DOWNS	90
50	NUMBER OF PUNTS	69
1976	TOTAL YARDS - PUNTS	2606
39.5	AVERAGE YARDS - PUNTS	37.7
61	NUMBER OF PENALTIES	58
580	YRDS. LOST ON PENALTIES	495
21	NUMBER OF FUMBLES	31
16	BALL LOST ON FUMBLES	18
43	TOUCHDOWNS	10
26	CONVERSIONS	8
2	SAFETY - AGAINST	1

"When the USF Dons left the stadium for the last time there was no parade, no endorsement deals for athletic shoes, power drinks or breakfast cereal; just a locker to be cleaned out and a train ride home to catch. But what they didn't know was that their lives would be changed forever because they had been part of something great; and greatness, no matter how brief, stays with a man. Every athlete dreams of a championship season - these men lived it."

—Paraphrased from the
Warner Bros. movie,
"The Replacements"
Gene Hackman's final speech.

CHAPTER SEVEN
Doers of the Deed

"Fifty years ago, we formed lifelong relationships. We're still like family."

—Fullback Burl Toler
50 year reunion - 2001

San Francisco Foghorn

OFFICIAL PUBLICATION OF THE ASSOCIATED STUDENTS

UNIVERSITY OF SAN FRANCISCO

SAN FRANCISCO, NOVEMBER 30, 1951

SEVENTEEN SENIORS GAVE USF ITS FINEST FOOTBALL TEAM

Ed Brown	Gino Marchetti	Lou Stephens
George Carley	Ollie Matson	Ralph Thomas
Ed Dawson	Mike Mergen	Burl Toler
Roy Giorgi	Merrill Peacock	Vince Tringali
Bill Henneberry	Hal Sachs	Bob Weibel
Greg Hillig	Vince Sakowski	

Time Runs Out On Matson, Men Who Blocked For Him

By: Walt Johnson

Time did what no opponent could do.

It finally defeated USF'S seniors of 1951, as it finally breaks down all great athletic teams.

Seventeen seniors suddenly found that their hourglass was still. Their breakneck speed was halted.

The stands are silent now, and the fog drifts quietly over an empty practice field. The equipment is stored away, and the chair is vacant behind Kuharich's desk.

They're being hailed as the finest football team in the University's history. This helps, but can't erase the loneliness they feel because of that missing "something" they thought such an essential part of their lives.

USF had become an ideal they sweated for, for which they blocked and tackled, and were sometimes crippled.

But they should feel joy in their accomplishments, not sadness in their memories.

Fame is often fleeting, but theirs will endure as long as there's a Fulton Street or a Green and Gold Room, a Campanile or a Gleeson Library.

*   *   *

In 1949, a young and heralded sophomore arrived on the Hilltop. He could run, and he could kick, but oh, how he could pass! In three subsequent seasons he more than lived up to his advance billing, but he became the most versatile man on a versatile ball club.

At 6'2" and 212, **Ed Brown** was big, and he ruined whole opposing teams with his big right arm. He tossed the pigskin short like a screaming rifle bullet, and heaved it down the field like a whistling artillery shell.

Sometimes he bootlegged, running like an out-of-control beer truck. On defense, he tackled as if he wanted to crack a concrete pillar.

A glance at his passing record shows the pros don't want the man from San Luis Obispo for throwing a javelin 190 feet.

*　*　*

This year's ROTC Cadet Colonel and alternate right halfback was bull-like **George Carley**, 187 pounds of snorting power. Sometimes called "Bonzo" because of his antics, Carley became strictly business on the field.

Uncle Sam will probably be calling this steady Eureka ball carrier in June.

*　*　*

Ed Dawson was the second fastest wingman on the squad, and a potentially fine receiver.

The 6'1", 193 pound end is a native of Santa Monica

He was particularly distinguished during Homecoming Week, escorting the Queen herself, Jean Kindy.

*　*　*

"Most underrated player in the Bay Area," was a tag hung on cornerlinebacker **Roy Giorgi**, a dark-haired San Franciscan.

He didn't have much of a chance to become "rated" playing the rest of his senior year only in spirit from a hospital bed and a wheel chair after a serious knee injury in the Fordham game.

A racehorse start enabled him to run four intercepted passes back for touchdowns during his Don Career. Though a good ball carrier, he was used almost exclusively to exploit his clever defensive tactics.

*　*　*

"Nineteen fifty-one is the year of "Quo Vadis," a saying undoubtedly originating from: "This is Henneberry's year."

In the waning moments of his junior year, the "Name" on the roster suddenly became president of the Block Club, and then emperor of a whole student body.

Bill Henneberry was a cunning field general behind Brown, and an excellent short passer. He "arrived" in a spring intrasquad game when he quarterbacked his team to an upset win. He reached the summit of his football career in the Camp Pendleton contest, directing a powerful ground offensive through a fierce opposing line as the Dons shut out the Marines, 26-0.

For this tribute to his craft, he received no credit from the village hacks, who seemed to think that touchdowns were chintzy if made by land.

Actually, he's a college reporter's dream, his accomplishments and "Henneberryisms" forming weekly subjects in news stories, sports articles or feature columns.

*   *   *

Through sheer ferociousness, 185 pound Guard **Greg Hillig** could drive back a man with a weight advantage of 25 pounds.

Around campus, the bespectacled Hillig resembled the "typical" biology student, but in a game looked entirely like a football player.

A swift downfield blocker from Cochrane, Wisconsin, he was also a hockey star in prep school.

*   *   *

Six feet, three inches and 225 pounds, arms like milk cartons and a torso like a Greek God. That was left tackle **Gino Marchetti**.

Called by Line Coach Bud Kerr, "the finest tackle I've ever coached." Marchetti, who almost outgrew the little town of Antioch, also became the best tackle on the Coast in his senior season.

Fastest lineman outside of the ends, Marchetti not only piled up plays to the inside, but also bashed down runners swinging wide.

Charging into the offensive backfields as if he were riding a horse, he abruptly trampled many pass plays before they even started.

His mates elected him co-captain before the start of the season.

*   *   *

Ollie Matson, the most accomplished footballer in USF history, shook off nicknames like he shook off tacklers.

"Elegant Ollie," they tried to call him. It didn't stick. Then it was "Matson Liner." Pretty fair, but just plain, "Ollie" surprised them both in catching the essence of the man.

Ambling through the corridors which his easy grin, he just didn't look "elegant," and hardly resembled a "liner." Yet a T-quarterback has never slammed the ball into the gut of a more lethal fullback.

But you know the Matson story thoroughly, a story without defects, of Matson the gridiron hero and Matson the man.

Other generations will gaze through a glass pane at the green jersey with the "33". No picture they form can possibly equal ours, who saw in person the man who wore that jersey, the epitome of the abbreviation "FB" in a football line-up.

* * *

At both tackle and guard, **Mike Mergen** stood out like the hulk of a ship. Here was Frank Norris' "Blond Superman." with hard leather pads stretched over his 6'5", 248 pound frame.

Opponents tried, but couldn't move him without a crane.

Mergen grew into a giant in McHenry, Illinois, and came West to have some fun squashing backs.

The impossible occurred in the COP game when everybody scrambled for a blocked punt that plunked into the Tiger end zone. Mergen finally collapsed on the ball for six points, and the thing didn't even burst.

* * *

Once hailed as the best prep back in the city, **Merrill Peacock** was shifted to end as a soph, and began racing under tosses far down the field.

He was the quickest flankman on the club, and a terrible threat to defensive secondaries, combining shiftiness with amazing catches.

* * *

Only one non-letterman appeared in the starting lineup. He was **Hal Sachs**, a 6'2", 200 pound Pasadenan.

The Dons were never forced to employ his field goal kicking to any great extent, and his rather polished public-speaking talents went almost entirely to waste.

He did remain the prime mover on play after play during the course of nine games.

* * *

Two Santa Clara men were just commencing a reverse following a Don punt when a streaking scatback belted over both of them

Vince Sakowski was an ideal "I" type halfback with explosive early speed. He shared the right half spot with Carley.

A walking sports encyclopedia from Shenandoah, Pennsylvania, Sakowski met with a sorry ending in the Loyola,contest, having two vertebrae cracked.

He is working for a teaching credential, majoring in history.

* * *

Lou Stephens probably showed more improvement than any player at USF in recent years.

He didn't even play football in high school, but a steady and conscientious spirit won him a position on the first team.

"Red" moved his 225 pounds from offensive right guard during his senior term, and was elected corresponding secretary of the student body.

*   *   *

Even when he first appeared out of Racine, Wisconsin, to enter the frosh squad lineup, **Ralph Thomas** was a blend of superb conditioning and extreme savageness.

A football makeup like this made him a type of player any coach would desire to have included on his roster.

He made few mistakes at either offensive or defensive end. Many of his catches came in the clutch, providing scores directly or indirectly.

The quiet, diligent Thomas' hobby was horticulture, a "human interest" element noted in a number of writeups during his career.

Recognizing his leadership even off the field, the student body selected him vice president, a post very similar to his stadium skills, embodying a lot of work with a little glory.

*   *   *

Kuharich hesitated, then scratched his bushy head. The blackboard was strewn with little "X's" representing the Dons, but there was a gaping hole in the defense.

Suddenly, he had the solution, as he said calmly, "Oh, Toler will cover that."

During three years, everywhere enemy runners were, **Burl Toler** also was. Just behind the line, far out on the flanks, or deep in the secondary, he operated like a scythe.

Tough to block, and tough to escape from, the Cleveland Browns already held the deed to this adhesive-like linebacker.

Co-Captain Toler, a lanky 210 pounder, filled out his full game at offensive tackle.

*   *   *

Vince Tringali, a San Franciscan, who put in two years of junior college ball at guard and tackle before entering USF, helped cement the middle of one of the country's most solid defensive lines.

He played the ukulele at squad vocal sessions.

*   *   *

Ordinarily quite amiable, **Bob Weibel** became one of the meanest characters in the game at his defensive end position.

He sometimes formed a ukulele duet with Tringali, and will have a June destination of Allentown, Pennsylvania, to become legend with the rest of his 1951 teammates.

*   *   *

ALL-AMERICAN OLLIE MATSON

"The winter rains struck the San Francisco peninsula, as they always do, and the Dons stayed inside, watching the films of their victory over College of the Pacific and waiting for the telephone operator to ring from Miami. They waited and they waited. They stayed in shape. The planned and they schemed. They saw pictures of the University of Kentucky's team. They dreamed gaudy dreams. No call ever came. No explanation was ever given."

—Wells Twombly
PRO! Magazine
November 11, 1973

8
CHAPTER EIGHT
EPILOGUE—A Season; An Era

"Undefeated, untied, and uninvited. You see you can't cry over spilled milk. When you know you're the best, what difference does it make?"

—Fullback Ollie Matson - 1951

Kezar Stadium

POST SEASON

San Francisco Chronicle

The City's Only Home-Owned Newspaper

FOUNDED 1865	SAN FRANCISCO. NOVEMBER, 1951	GA 1-1112

THE ORANGE
Mayor Gets In Plug For USF

Mayor Elmer E. Robinson yesterday made a pitch on behalf of the University of San Francisco for a bid to the Orange Bowl when he dispatched the following telegram:

Van C. Kussrow,
Orange Bowl Selection Committee
Miami,

As Mayor of San Francisco, I heartily recommend the selection of the University of San Francisco as the Orange Bowl opponent for Georgia Tech. I can assure you that San Francisco's only university has fielded a team this year of which we are very proud. You know the record it has compiled as a team. The selection of USF will provide the Orange Bowl classic with a team that is spirited and spectacular. It would be a great gesture on the part of the selection committee if the friendly rivalry which exists between Florida and California could be carried over into the Orange Bowl by the selection of the University of San Francisco.

(signed) Elmer E. Robinson, Mayor

(CHRONICLE EDITOR'S NOTE: Some San Franciscans have wondered whether the presence of two Negro stars – Ollie Matson and Burl Toler – on the USF squad would mitigate the Dons' chances to be invited to the Orange Bowl. USF has been informed that would not be so. Iowa used five Negroes against Miami U. in a regular season game in the Orange Bowl last year).

*   *   *

San Francisco Foghorn

OFFICIAL PUBLICATION OF THE ASSOCIATED STUDENTS

UNIVERSITY OF SAN FRANCISCO

SAN FRANCISCO, NOVEMBER 30, 1951

Bowl Excuse Is Weak

By: Al Schlarmann
    USF Sports Editor
    (excerpt regarding football team's loss at bowl bid)

It's final now. There will be no bowl bid for the Don football team this January 1. The greatest football team in the history of this university has played its last game as a unit and all that remains now is a bright memory. This issue of the FOGHORN, therefore, is dedicated to those seventeen seniors, and especially Ollie Matson, who trudged into the locker room in the Rose Bowl after last Sunday's game and took off their Green jerseys for the final time.

Most of the students feel worse about those four yards by which Matson missed the national collegiate rushing record than does Ollie himself. Walking off the field, the great fullback acted more like he'd dropped a nickel than a chance for immortality, and his first concern was for his teammates who had helped him gain his All-American status this year. On and off the field for the past three years, Ollie has never let his successes affect him.

The great Negro fullback is USF's first football All-American and for this reason, if for no other, his big number 33 should be retired to the trophy case. If the New York Yankees baseball team with their long list of star performers could afford to so honor two of their immortals, Babe Ruth and Lou Gehrig, then the Dons should feel bound to do the same for Ollie.

We predicted before the start of the season that, because of their weak schedule, USF would not be invited to a major post-season bowl regardless of their record. If the Orange Bowl committee legislated against the Dons for this reason alone, and not because of any discrimination, we have to accept their decision as an honest one; but we cannot understand why they had to stir up a lot of unnecessary excitement and hope in these quarters for no reason at all. They knew our schedule three weeks ago when they first announced that USF was being considered as a contender. Why, then, at the end of an undefeated season, should they drop us from the list for a reason that could have more validly been used to overlook us from the beginning?

*   *   *

Meanwhile, USF Coach Joe Kuharich said the Dons have received an "unofficial feeler" regarding their interest in playing in the Salad Bowl in Phoenix, Ariz., New Year's Day.

Kuharich added, however, that any post-season game bids are up to the university's administration. Furthermore, Kuharich commented that he doubted seriously whether the squad "would be interested" in playing in the Salad Bowl.

Although written in November of 1990, six months prior to the team's fortieth reunion, in an article for *Sports Illustrated*, Ron Fimrite summed up that magical season best -

November 12, 1990   # SPORTS ILLUSTRATED

BEST TEAM YOU NEVER HEARD OF (excerpt)
The '51 Dons were unbeaten - and unsung

By: Ron Fimrite

The 51 team had become the first in USF football history to finish a season undefeated. The Dons had risen from obscurity to make a name for themselves. Their big line, anchored by Marchetti, St. Clair and Mergen, had held USF's opponents to a net rushing average of 51.6 yards per game over the nine-game season. Matson had led the nation with 1,566 yards rushing, four short of Texas Mines' (now University of Texas, El Paso) Fred Wendt's 1948 record for a single season, and with 21 touchdowns, one shy of the 1950 record that was shared by Nebraska's Bobby Reynolds and Arizona State's Wilford White. He had made touchdown runs of 94, 90, 68, 67, 54, 46 and 45 yards.

The Dons boarded Southern Pacific's Daylight train home from Los Angeles on Monday morning after the Loyola win. They were convinced that a bowl bid was awaiting them back home, so the party started the moment the train pulled out of the station. Vince Tringali on ukulele and guard Dick Colombini on accordion played endless choruses of *Up a Lazy River* and the team's theme song, *Good Night, Irene.*

"They ran out of beer by Santa Barbara," recalled backup quarterback Bill Henneberry. "Even the normally reserved Kuharich joined in the revelry, raising a glass to the greatest season he would ever have."

As the party wound down, Henneberry and Matson talked. "Ollie had such a quiet emotional attachment to those guys," Henneberry remembered. "He told me he'd had offers to go to schools all over the country. He had chosen USF because no place was friendlier, no place made him feel so wanted. It was like a speech after the last battle."

The train reached the Third and Townsend Street station in San Francisco at about six o'clock that evening. "We were expecting a big crowd to meet us, but there was only a handful of people on the platform," said Henneberry. "We wondered why there weren't more there to share in our jubilation. And then, as we stepped off the train, we heard the devastating news: Georgia Tech and Baylor would be playing in the Orange Bowl. All of the major bowls, except the Rose and the Sun, in El Paso, would entertain Southern teams only. Pacific, trounced by the Dons, would go to the Sun Bowl."

"You could've heard a pin drop in that station" said Matson.

The announced reason for rejecting USF was its soft schedule. But San Francisco sportscaster, Ira Blue, reported that he was told by Gator Bowl President Sam Wolfson that the Gator, Sugar and Orange Bowl committees had all decided to avoid teams with "Negro players." There was an intimation that had the Dons had been willing to play without Matson and Toler, they might have been extended a bid. This was out of the question. "What I think we should have done, says (halfback) Joe Scudero, is send Ollie and Burl to one of those bowls and leave the rest of us home. Hell, the two of them could have beaten most of those Southern schools by themselves."

*   *   *

San Francisco Chronicle **EXTRA**

The City's Only Home-Owned Newspaper

FOUNDED 1865   SAN FRANCISCO. NOVEMBER, 1951   GA 1-1112

USF QUITS FOOTBALL
Loyola of L. A. Also Drops Game

USF, Loyola Quit Game Simultaneously
Kerr Still Has Job; 'Concerned Over Kids'

By: Bill Anderson

University of San Francisco and Loyola of Los Angeles dealt intercollegiate football another heavy blow today when their presidents announced, simultaneously, their decisions to abandon the sport.

It is rather ironic that USF should be forced to the wall at a time when it finally had achieved the prestige it had sought so long.

Father William J. Dunne, S.J., USF's president, said he was "very unhappy" to have to make the announcement. An ardent sports lover, Father Dunne said the game would be continued on an intramural level but that "for small universities and colleges such as ours, the game has become too much a part of the entertainment world, too great and costly a spectacle, to be maintained."

Father Dunne said the decision by Loyola to also quit the sport was not a part of a general withdrawal from football by Jesuit institutions. Ours was a local matter as was Loyola's, he said. "However, the decision to make simultaneous announcements was not a coincidence. We agreed to do that."

Santa Clara University, another Jesuit school, made a denial through Athletic Director Denny Heenan that it was considering dropping the game.

Broncos Will Play

"We will definitely continue with football," Heenan said. "There has been no talk or consideration of dropping it."

Rumors, given impetus by former USF Coach Joe Kuharich's frank statement on the situation some time back, that the Jesuit order was withdrawing from football, were denied by Father Dunne.

"It is an individual matter," he said. "Other Jesuit schools such as Cincinnati, Detroit, Boston College and Holy Cross are able to maintain the sport financially. We cannot. Our primary obligation is to promote the efficiency of academic processes. Present world conditions have created an abnormal strain on private colleges and universities.

"In our own case, the recent developments of the graduate division, introduction of new credentials in the teacher training program, the general strengthening of faculty personnel and the inauguration of research projects have vastly increased the operating cost of the university over the past few years.

Eight Jesuits Left

"To maintain, therefore, an extra curricular activity such as football, which seems to be incompatible to adjustment under present conditions, would be financially imprudent."

Still, it should be noted there are now but eight of 27 Jesuit colleges engaged in football. Georgetown, Canisius, Buffalo and Gonzaga are others which have dropped the sport in recent years.

St. Mary's is not a Jesuit school. But all these which have dropped the sport are the small ones which cannot compete with larger institutions in the matter of scholarships, travel and guarantees for schedules.

Bud Kerr, recently recommended successor to Kuharich as football coach at USF, said he was not depressed although the final exploding of his hopes to coach a college football team was a blow.

"I knew there was some doubt as to whether we would be able to continue the game," Kerr said. "However, Father Dunne told me at the time he would do everything he could to keep it going. I know he was sincere but he had not yet been able to look over the financial report or confer with the board of trustees.

Concern for Kids

"My main concern," Kerr added, "is with the kids - such as Joe Scudero and Bob St. Clair. It will be a shock to them. Football is a major part of their college careers. Any boy who is a fine athlete wants to use his talents and dropping the sport hurts them a great deal.

"I believe these boys should be allowed to transfer, without loss of credit or eligibility to schools where they could continue to play the game they love. To many of them, it is as much a part of school as English or mathematics or history. And I believe they learn a great deal from the sport. Some want to become physical education teachers or coaches and their opportunities for such positions are jeopardized by such tragedies as this."

Kerr, himself, had no great worries for his own position.

*   *   *

𝕾𝖆𝖓 𝕵𝖗𝖆𝖓𝖈𝖎𝖘𝖈𝖔 𝕰𝖝𝖆𝖒𝖎𝖓𝖊𝖗

Monarch of the Dailies

MONDAY, DECEMBER 31, 1951

Kuharich: 'Tragedy'
No Other Choice, Ex-Coach Says

By: Dick Toner

Men connected with the 1951 football picture at University of San Francisco reacted in varying manners yesterday to the news that the sport had been abandoned on the Hilltop.

Joe Kuharich, who coached the Dons through the school's first unbeaten season this year and then resigned, called the discontinuance "quite a tragedy."

Some players were shocked. Others adopted a fatalistic attitude. All of them expressed surprise.

NO CHOICE

Kuharich said he had seen the move coming, though he had heard no inkling of the action until it was taken.

"It's quite a tragedy, no question about it," said Kuharich. "But I can't help but be honest and say I felt it was inevitable. It was a matter of time. The university was backed into a corner. It had no choice."

SCHEDULE PROBLEM

Laying blame for the development on scheduling difficulties and pointing mutely at Pacific Coast Conference universities, Kuharich said:

"It's a sad story when a university of that caliber (USF) can't compete against major schools in games it needs to keep its football program going.

"There's no doubt inability to arrange suitable schedules forced the abandonment. Even big intersectional opponents wouldn't do. USF had to have enough games against powers in the general area. As has been related before, it couldn't get them."

VOICES CONCERN

The former Don mentor was concerned with the plight of the gridders at USF with remaining eligibility.

"It's most unfortunate for them," he remarked. "Boys like Bob St. Clair, Joe Scudero, Frank McLaughlin and Jim Whitney are good football players. Now college football careers are ended for some, and others will lose eligibility if they transfer. Maybe some prospective professional careers will have been nipped in the bud.

"For instance, St. Clair and Scudero, who lose their senior year of eligibility, are outstanding. St. Clair is of All America caliber and I think Scudero might have the ability to make a good pro halfback.

"How can they prove it now?"

Kuharich, head coach at USF for four years, again denied he had resigned because of pre-knowledge the university would not field a team in 1952.

"YOU'RE KIDDING"

One player's attitude was voiced by Senior Bill Henneberry, student body president and reserve quarterback. Hearing of the university's decision for the first time when contacted for comment, he said:

"You're kidding!...

"Well, that's really a shock. It'll be tough on Bud Kerr (new coach), Jim Ryan (assistant coach) and the players with eligibility. It was completely unexpected to me and I feel awfully bad about it.

"It'll hurt the student body because football always is a morale factor. But, then, I guess it couldn't be helped."

Sophomore Leo Madden, a promising 195 pound guard from Omaha, Nebraska indicated he would transfer and said:

"From what I've heard, most of the players with eligibility will prefer to go elsewhere so they can play some more football, even though they lose a year.

"I've heard the university will keep the scholarships in effect. But I'd still like to play football.

"Probably I'll go back to the Midwest," he declared resignedly.

Joe Arenivar, a brilliant freshman halfback who suffered a broken collar bone in the Fordham game, said the announcement "hit me pretty hard."

"I want to play football. But before I make any plans I'll talk to Coach Kerr," said the Pittsburg youngster.

Merrill Peacock, senior end: "What? They dropped football? It's news to me. And a surprise. Too bad. Guess I finished just in time."

St. Clair: "It was a shock. I still can't realize it's true. One thing, I guess it'll keep me from realizing my greatest ambition, playing in the Shrine game. Yes, I did count strongly on playing pro ball." (St. Clair is married and has a daughter.)

Jim Kearney, junior halfback: "We players will get along. But I feel sorry for Kerr and Ryan. They were rarin' to go and would have had a good team next year. It's the biggest blow to football around here."

*   *   *

San Francisco Examiner

Monarch of the Dailies

Tulsa Lands St. Clair;
Don Backs 'Unheeded'

By: Bill Mulligan
    Copy Editor–Sports

Junior, sophomore and freshmen football players on the USF varsity squad last fall are finding it extremely difficult to get into other college unless they are rugged, experienced linemen, Coach Bud Kerr reported yesterday.

Since USF quit football early this month Kerr has been trying to get his charges into other institutions on athletic scholarships but without too much luck.

Kerr says that no school seems interested in backfield men, even such an outstanding one as little Joe Scudero, who has one year of eligibility left.

Bob St. Clair, 6-7, 235 pound offensive end and defensive tackle, is the only one definitely placed. He will transfer to Tulsa University. Harmon Welsh, 218 pound sophomore guard, also will probably end up at the Oklahoma school. John Dwyer, 185 pound guard, and Tim Moriarity, 220 pound guard, may go to Detroit U. If not, they also are probable Tulsa transfers.

ONE BACK GETS BID

Tulsa may take Bill Dando, 185 pound halfback from Gordon, Pa. He is the only back that has received any offer from a major school.

Frank McLaughlin, senior, and Tom Montero, sophomore, both ends; Jim Whitney, back; Joe Arenivar; back; Joe DeBernardi, guard; John Holm, good freshman end prospect, and Bob Schaeffer, guard, probably, will remain at USF as they are in the school of business administration.

Gene Chess, flashy little freshman back, wants to go to Detroit.

John Cronan, sophomore quarterback, Bob Springer, halfback; Jack Becker, guard, and Dick Arnoldi, end, may enter San Francisco State College.

Coach Joe Verducci has extended them an invitation to transfer there.

Holm, a San Francisco boy, also may go to State.

Frank Monti, point after touchdown, kickoff and field goal specialist, did not return to USF after Christmas. Jim Boggan, halfback from Willows, California also has dropped out of school.

EYES MIDWEST SCHOOL

Fullback Dick Huxley, Roy Bruna, center; Walter Thiel, back; Larry Slajchert and Walter Roland, quarterbacks, and Dick Columbini, guard, are still in school and have no offers from other institutions.

Leo Madden, guard, wants to try for a midwest school. He is from Omaha. His father died last season and he moved his mother to San Francisco. Now that USF is out of football he would like to move back to the midwest and attend a college engaging in the gridiron sport.

LINEMAN WANTED

"Most of the boys who have had no offers from other schools will probably stay at USF until June and find other locations during the summer months," Kerr said.

"I will try to place them where I think they will fit in and be happy. Scudero may line up at Tulsa. Whitney, too, may go either to Detroit or Tulsa. But backs are seemingly not wanted. Big, tough linemen are in demand. In fact, Oklahoma A & M, after listening to my pleas, telegraphed me they were sorry but couldn't use any of the USF players.

"What about myself? Well, I have several irons in the fire. But mainly I am making business inquiries here. If I can't get a head coaching job, I would much rather stay in the San Francisco area and work as salesman or in some line of public relations."

*   *   *

The Call Bulletin

JOE'S THOUGHTS WITH HIS GREAT 1951 TEAM AS HE DEPARTS HILLTOP

By: Jack McDonald
    Sports Editor

USF not only loses a very competent football coach but a fine man - loyal, conscientious and decent - in Joe Kuharich. In 1948 he took over a flock of players who had transferred from other colleges spread all over the country. The personnel was packed with disillusioned malcontents. It was the toughest job in all college football, bar none.

But patiently Kuharich set about fashioning a team which was to prove the first unbeaten eleven in Hilltopper history. Nobody will ever know how great a team it may have been for it never got the chance to test itself against a strong, major opponent.

Even as Kuharich was confirming his resignation yesterday, at a time when he could certainly be excused for having his own future uppermost in his mind, Joe's thoughts were solely with his 1951 boys, whose greatness he has never doubted.

For a good half hour he sat expanding on the virtues of his unbeaten 1951 Hilltoppers.

"If I never field another winner in my life I'll feel my career as a coach was a success just for having directed this one," Joe began, feelingly. "It hustled. It was durable. It was determined. It liked to play football. It wouldn't be denied. Its greatest asset was that it had one thing in mind - to go unbeaten.

"I never expect again to coach a squad that will work together as this 1951 USF team. Not a boy on this squad was the least bit jealous of the other fellow's popularity. Honestly, I cannot say that Toler, Brown, Marchetti and Scudero weren't just as deserving of All American recognition as Ollie Matson.

But we knew a small school like ours would be lucky to land one man on an All America team. Everybody on the team knew this and worked unselfishly to make Matson the one.

"Scudero, at a great personal sacrifice, let Matson do most of the ball carrying. Joe is a great runner himself and has that electrifying way of running that stimulates a crowd. He knew he would get his chance next season, and willingly and unselfishly gave way to Ollie."

"And take Lou Stephens, one of our guards." went on Kuharich. "It was his blocking that shook Matson loose so many times. He got little public recognition for it, but the movies show the great blocking he did to make Ollie the leading scorer of the nation and one of the biggest ground-gainers of all time.

"And Hillig, our other guard. He weighs only 178, and wears contact lenses. Had no high school experience. He was as fine and tough a football player as we had."

Had Perfect Attitude

We broke in here to ask Kuharich what his chances were of landing the Chicago Cardinal coaching job. He didn't even hear us!

*   *   *

Twelve of the Dons, from both the 1950 and 1951 teams (as well as their Athletic Publicist), were soon to meet again as they made their mark on the National Football League.

CHAPTER NINE
Next Stop: the NFL

"If we had an expansion franchise, I would start it with just that team. They were so great!"

—Pete Rozelle - 1991
Former NFL Commissioner and
1951 USF Athletic Publicist

San Francisco Chronicle

The City's Only Home-Owned Newspaper

FOUNDED 1865   SAN FRANCISCO. WEDNESDAY, MARCH 6, 1968   421-1112

Glimpse Into Grid Past
Dons Stocked the Pros

By: Darrell Wilson
        Sportswriter

In 1950, Stanford defeated USF's next to last football team, 55-7.

Dick Friendlich, the Stanford graduate who covered the game for the Sporting Green said, kindly enough, "The Indians got the jump on them"

Pierre Salinger, a USF graduate and also a Chronicle reporter at the time, complained, "Stanford poured it on."

Pete Rozelle, the USF publicist, said, "We'll get them next year."

Stanford had a pretty good team in 1950 (5-3-2). but hindsight indicates that the Dons (7-4) should have done a better job.

Consider the facts. Eleven members of that USF team played a total of 85 years in the NFL during a period when professional football consisted of only 12 teams in one league, instead of the present 26 clubs in two leagues.

These 11 USF grads were among the greatest players in the history of all football. They were named All Pro a total of 25 years and played in so many Pro Bowl games that the mind reels counting how many.

The 1951 team which, naturally, followed the 1950 group, contained all the eventual NFL stars except Dick Stanfel and the late Roy Barni. This 1951 crew went undefeated, but the soft schedule didn't contain Stanford, California or any other top ranked club.

Joe Kuharich coached both the 1950 and 1951 clubs, and it is certain that his groups contained a larger percentage of top pro players than that of any other team in history.

These were the USF pros: Fullback Ollie Matson, who played for 16 years, was All Pro five times while with a very weak Chicago Cardinal team which seldom won. Although not as spectacular as San Francisco's Hugh McElhenny, Ollie was generally regarded as the top running back of his era.

Gino Marchetti, 13 years, is regarded as the best defensive end who has ever played the game (David Jones, currently with the Rams, is usually rated second). Gino was All Pro for nine years and was in 10 straight Pro Bowl games while starring with Baltimore's championship teams.

Bob St. Clair, who was a gangling 6-9 offensive end (and defensive tackle) on USF's 1951 team, played 12 years with the San Francisco 49ers. He was selected All Pro offensive tackle three times, was in five Pro Bowl games and would have lasted two or three more years except for a ruptured Achilles tendon.

Stanfel was a Detroit All Pro five times in his short seven year span as an NFL offensive guard. Dick is now Kuharich's assistant coach with the Philadelphia Eagles.

Quarterback Ed Brown, perhaps the best known for his ability to burn candles, nevertheless played 15 years in the NFL, mostly with Chicago. Ed liked to participate in fun and games, especially at the famous Bear parties, but he was a tough football player who made the Pro Bowl in 1956 and 1957. And those who saw the Bears ruin San Francisco's title hopes in 1954 will remember Ed's 60 yard pass to Harlon Hill for the winning touchdown in the last seconds.

Barni was a five year defensive back with various clubs; Louis (Red) Stephens was a rugged NFL guard for six seasons, and Joe Scudero was a combination punt returner and defensive back for six years.

Guard Mike Mergen and receiver Ralph Thomas each played two years with the Cardinals, and receiver Merrill Peacock was with the Cards in 1952.

Burl Toler, USF's 1950-1951 center, was regarded as Matson's equal as a pro prospect. But Burl was injured in the College All Star game and was never able to play pro football. He is now a San Francisco teacher and an NFL official.

*   *   *

University of San Francisco
1950 and 1951 Team Stats with the
National Football League

1951 Team Drafted by the Pros (10)

Ed Brown:	Chicago Bears, Pittsburgh Steelers, and 1 game with the Baltimore Colts
Gino Marchetti:	New York Yankees, Dallas Texans and Baltimore Colts.
Ollie Matson:	Chicago Cardinals, Los Angeles Rams, Detroit Lions and Philadelphia Eagles
Mike Mergen:	Chicago Cardinals
Merrill Peacock:	Chicago Cardinals
Bob St. Clair:	San Francisco 49ers
Joe Scudero:	Toronto Argonauts (Canadian Football League), Washington Redskins, and Pittsburgh Steelers
Lou Stephens:	Chicago Cardinals and Washington Redskins
Ralph Thomas:	Chicago Cardinals and Washington Redskins
Burl Toler:	Drafted by Cleveland Browns in Junior year at USF, but traded to Chicago Cardinals before '52 season began. Hurt in '52 All Star Game. Never played pro ball, but served 25 years as a National Football League official.
Pete Rozelle:	Public Relations Director for the Los Angeles Rams and upon death of Burt Bell, became Commissioner of the National Football League.
Joe Kuharich:	Coached Chicago Cardinals, Washington Redskins and Philadelphia Eagles.

1950 Team Drafted By the Pros (2)

Dick Stanfel:	Detroit Lions and Washington Redskins
Roy Barni:	Chicago Cardinals, Philadelphia Eagles and Washington Redskins

A total of **twelve** players were drafted from both the 1950 and 1951 teams. All twelve players were members of the 1950 team.

Pro Football Hall of Fame

Gino Marchetti and Ollie Matson - Class of 1972. USF is the only college in collegiate football history to have two players from the same team inducted into the Hall of Fame at the same time. The other two members from the 51 team were:

Bob St. Clair - Class of 1990

Pete Rozelle (team athletic publicist) - Class of 1993

Pro Bowl

January 15, 1956

Six players from both the 1950 and 1951 teams played in the 1956 Pro Bowl.

Ed Brown - Chicago Bears

Gino Marchetti - Baltimore Colts

Ollie Matson - Chicago Cardinals

Joe Scudero - Washington Redskins

Bob St. Clair - San Francisco 49ers

Dick Stanfel - Detroit Lions

Pro Bowl Appearances

Ed Brown - 2

Gino Marchetti - 11

Ollie Matson - 5

Joe Scudero - 1

Bob St. Clair - 5

Dick Stanfel - 5

Total Pro Bowl Appearances by both the 50 and 51 Teams - 29

All NFL

Gino Marchetti - 57–62 and 64 (7)

Ollie Matson - 54–57 (4)

Bob St. Clair - 55–57 (3)

All Millennium

Gino Marchetti - Defensive Tackle - Baltimore Colts

All Decade

Bob St. Clair - Offensive Tackle - San Francisco 49ers

Dick Stanfel - Defensive Guard - Detroit Lions and Washington Redskins

*   *   *

THE 1951 DONS: AN NFL BONANZA

December 30, 1977

Author unknown

In 1951 Frank Gifford was 21 and a campus idol at USC. Hugh McElhenny was making his dazzling runs for the University of Washington.

Cal, with Les Richter and Johnny Olszewski, and Stanford, with Bill McColl and Gary Kerkorian, were both national powers; and while Cal won the Big Game, Stanford went to the Rose Bowl.

It was a vintage year for college football. The NFL draft would produce such longtime stars as Bill George, Ray Renfro, Billy Howton, Vito (Babe) Parilli and Dick (Night Train) Lane.

At the time, the University of San Francisco appeared to be just another good team on the West Coast; a pity, the experts said, that the Dons played such a soft schedule. It diminished the significance of their unbeaten record and denied them their goal: the Orange Bowl.

In retrospect, however, USF, in its last year of big time football, might have been the greatest college team of all time, one which missed its only chance for a bowl game not because of its schedule, but racial prejudice.

The Dons averaged 36 points per game, overpowering their opposition. The Dons' 8th game against COP was their most important. They were led to believe that a strong showing would make them a prime candidate for the Orange Bowl. COP was leading the nation with an average of 344 yards rushing per game, and many observers felt the Tigers' Eddie Macon would outshine Matson before a sellout crowd in Stockton.

It was no contest. Matson out rushed Macon 175 to 80; and the Dons destroyed COP 47-14. Yet the Orange Bowl remained unimpressed. The bid went to the Southwest Conference team, Baylor (against Georgia Tech), and the headlines read: USF: Unbeaten, Untied and Uninvited.

"The Dons are not well enough known here," a spokesman said. "Their schedule was just too weak We suggest they add some big name opponents next year."

But there was more to it than that. Santa Clara, on the same scale with USF in national publicity, had gone to the Orange Bowl only two years earlier.

Asked about it today, the team's black stars, Matson and Toler, hint that racial prejudice was the determining factor. "Times were a lot different then," Matson said, "and I'm sure the racial thing entered into it."

"I don't think there's any doubt," St. Clair said. "That's the way things were in the South. When I got to the pros there were times when the (49er) black players couldn't stay at the hotel. They were farmed out to private families. I think we could have gone to Miami without Ollie and Burl, but there's no way we would have wanted that. We were together in every sense of the word. That's one of the reasons we were great."

*   *   *

𝔓𝔯𝔬 𝔉𝔬𝔬𝔱𝔟𝔞𝔩𝔩 𝔚𝔢𝔢𝔨𝔩𝔶

Pro Football History: The 1951 Dons
University of San Francisco was unusual football factory

By: Jim Campbell

July 26, 1999

With apologies to Tony Bennett, the 1951 University of San Francisco football team left its impression on the hearts of many in the "City by the Bay." The Dons, once described as "a track star (Ollie Matson) and some local toughs (Gino Marchetti and Joe Scudero)," became victims of their own success. The green and gold finished the season undefeated, but the high cost of operating a big-time football program at a small college took its toll. USF dropped football after that outstanding season.

What makes the team noteworthy are the three Pro Football Hall of Fame players it produced. Marchetti, Matson and Bob St. Clair are enshrined in the Canton, Ohio museum. But there's more to the story. This trio was joined in the NFL by eight teammates and their head coach, Joe Kuharich.

Still not enough? The athletic news director was Alvin Rozelle, a.k.a. Pete - the future commissioner of the NFL.

Want more? The best player on the team, by consensus of his teammates, was Burl Toler, who got hurt in the college All Star Game and missed out on an NFL playing career. Toler, however, did work in the league with skill and dignity as a head lineman. He was the league's first African-American official.

This group had little difficulty completing a perfect 9-0 season. Bill Henneberry, a quarterback and now director of athletic development at his alma mater, said, "We won by an average score of 33-8."

Once the game was in hand, the students let the opponents know it. Taking a cue from a popular folk song, with the USF band accompanying, they would sing, "Irene, good night, Irene, good night, Good night, Irene," as they waved their handkerchiefs. With no on-campus facilities, the team played in venerable Kezar Stadium.

Unable to meet the mounting costs, and missing out on a bowl game - there were rumors the Orange bowl committee was interested, but it never sent an invitation - the sport was discontinued.

Kuharich was tapped to coach the Chicago Cardinals. Kuharich, in turn, tapped Matson in the first round of the draft. Matson, who led the nation in scoring (126 points) and rushing (1,566 yards), reported to camp late. He was occupied in Helsinki, Finland, winning Olympic bronze in the 400 meters and silver with the 4 x 400 relay team.

Kuharich, whose NFL record never equaled what he did at USF, brought other Dons to Chicago. Roy Barni, a textbook tackler off the 1950 team, played defensive back for the Cardinals. Mike Mergen, a rugged tackle, also joined Kuharich. So did end Merrill Peacock. The other end, Ralph Thomas, was also a '52 Cardinal member.

Others went elsewhere, mainly via the NFL draft. Marchetti, the prototype of today's pass rushing defensive end, actually served a year with the Dallas Texans before the franchise move to Baltimore. Not realizing exactly what they had, the Texans played the future fast food millionaire at offensive tackle. With the Colts, Marchetti formed the nucleus of championship teams in 1958 and 1959. He was selected to the NFL's all time team in 1969 and again in 1994 as the NFL celebrated its 75th season.

Dick Stanfel, worthy of inclusion in the Hall of Fame - he's come close on occasion - debuted with the Lions in 1952. Stanfel broke the mold. He was the first big, rangy (6' 3", 236 pounds) guard. Most guards in that era were short and squat.

Stanfel played magnificently on Lions title teams of the 1950's. He remained in the NFL as a valued assistant for decades and was a member of the Saints' staff as recently as the '97 season.

St. Clair transferred to Tulsa after the Dons disbanded, but the 6 foot 9 offensive tackle couldn't hide from the hometown 49ers, who selected him in the third round of the 1953 draft. The All Pro was used also on goal line defense and blocked 10 field goals in 1956.

Ed Brown made his NFL debut in 1954. The smooth throwing quarterback led the Bears to the 1956 title game and played a dozen seasons.

Offensive guard Lou Stephens, who didn't pick up the nickname "Red" until he got to the NFL, was reunited with Kuharich in 1955 with the Redskins after fulfilling a Korean War military obligation.

Scudero lived up to his nickname "Scooter" as a kick returner and defensive back. The 170 pound whippet gained 1,738 yards on returns in a six year career.

After a rookie season that saw Matson take two of his 20 kickoff returns all the way for touchdowns, he became one of the most feared and coveted players in the league. He was truly something special, Scudero said, "he was the first really big, big back who would run with sprinter's speed. His Olympic medals prove that."

While the Cardinals were going nowhere, Matson was going everywhere. He rushed for 924 yards in 1956, when the 12 game schedule made 1000 yards a true milestone. The next season Matson averaged 22.6 yards on 20 catches. Prior to that, in 1955 he led the NFL in punt return yards (245) an average (18.8). In 1958, he averaged a league-leading 35.5 yards on kickoff returns.

When Matson was acquired (for nine players) by the Rams in '59, he responded with 853 rushing yards but was later mismanaged. Because of his versatility, Rams coaches used, or misused him as a tight end, defensive back and flanker. His ability remained, but his numbers fell off. Still, Matson racked up 760 all around yards for Kuharich with the Eagles in '64.

Matson, an eloquent spokesman for the team, summoned up the feelings of the talent laden dons, who received relatively little recognition outside of the Bay Area. Said Matson, "Undefeated, untied, uninvited. You see, you can't cry over spilled milk. When you know you're the best - what difference does it make.

*   *   *

Although the Kuharich Era at USF had ended, the successes of the players, themselves, had just begun. The following is a chronological outline on those individuals who made it to the National Football League.

Chicago Cardinals coach Joe Kuharich with his former USF players who are now members of his Cardinals team. From left (standing), Ollie Matson, Mike Mergan, Coach Kuharich, and Merrill Peacock.
Front row: Roy Barni, Don Panciera, and Ralph Thomas

ROY BARNI
Halfback - 5' 11" 185 lbs
- Joined the Chicago Cardinals in 1952
- Signed with the Philadelphia Eagles in 1954
- Joined Washington Redskins in 1955
- 5 days before reporting to camp for Redskins 57 campaign, Barni was shot and killed while breaking up a fight in his tavern, 'The Huddle' on San Francisco's Telegraph Hill.

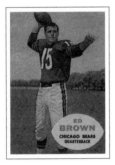

ED BROWN
Quarterback/Defensive Back - 6' 2" 220 lbs
- Drafted by the Chicago Bears while still in the Marine Corps in 1952
- Came into the league in 1954
- Led the Bears in punting for six straight seasons
- Leading passer in five of the last six seasons
- 1956 first quarterback in Bear history to lead the NFL in passing
- Selected to the Pro Bowl in 1956 and 1957
- Traded to Pittsburgh Steelers in 1961
- Comeback Player of the Year in 1963
- Retired from the NFL in 1965

MIKE MERGEN
Tackle - 6' 5" 248 lbs
- Drafted by the Chicago Cardinals in 1952
- 27 year career in law enforcement upon leaving the NFL

MERRILL PEACOCK

End - 6' 0" 185 lbs

- Drafted by the Chicago Cardinals in 1952

JOE SCUDERO

Halfback - 5' 10" 165 lbs

- In 1953 he played for the Toronto Argonauts of the Canadian Football League
- Earned All League honors in '53
- In 1954 he played for the Washington Redskins
- Selected to Pro Bowl in 1956
- In 1960 he played one year for the Pittsburgh Steelers

DICK STANFEL

Guard - 6' 3" 236 lbs

- 1953 – Drafted by the Detroit Lions
- 1953 – Lions MVP
- 1952 and 1953 – Lions are World Champions
- 1954 – Lions win Division
- 1953 and 1954 – All Pro/Pro Bowl
- 1958 – Traded to Washington Redskins and voted to three consecutive Pro Bowls
- 1959-1962 – Line coach under Joe Kuharich - Notre Dame
- 1963 – Line coach under Marv Levy - University of California at Berkeley
- 1964-1970 – Line coach under Joe Kuharich - Philadelphia Eagles

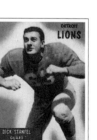

- 1971-1975 – Line coach under Dick Nolan – San Francisco Forty Niners
- 1975 – Coached Pro Bowl in Hawaii
- 1976-1980 – Line coach under Hank Stram – New Orleans Saints
- 1981-1992 – Line coach under Mike Ditka.
- 1984 – Bears won Division Championship, Coached All Pro game
- 1985 – Bears won Division Championship
- 1986 – Bears are Super Bowl Champions
- 1993 – Retired from the NFL
- 1996 – Named "Guard of the Decade" in Sports Illustrated"s Silver Anniversary, 'Teams of the Decades 1950-1960.
- 1997-1999 – Brought out of retirement by Mike Ditka to line coach New Orleans Saints.
- 2001 – Chosen as one of six Charter Enshrinees into the East-West Shrine Game's Hall of Fame

Lou Stephens
Washington Redskins   Guard

LOU "RED" STEPHENS

Guard - 6' 0" 225 lbs

- In 1953 he played and coached one season of Army football
- Drafted by the Chicago Cardinals 1952
- Free agent – signed by Washington Redskins in 1955
- All Pro Honorable Mention in 1955 and 1960
- Retired from football in 1960
- Coached with Joe Kuharich at Notre Dame from 1961-1963.

RALPH THOMAS

End - 5' 11" 193 lbs

Ralph Thomas
Washington Redskins   End

- Free agent - signed by the Chicago Cardinals in 1952
- Entered Army and named to the 1953 and 1954 All Army Football Teams
- Joined the Washington Redskins in 1955
- Player of the Week in 1955 – against Philadelphia Eagles and New York Giants
- Still holds NFL record for quickest touchdown scored between touchdowns – under five seconds (Redskins vs. Eagles, September 1955)
- Retired from the NFL in 1956

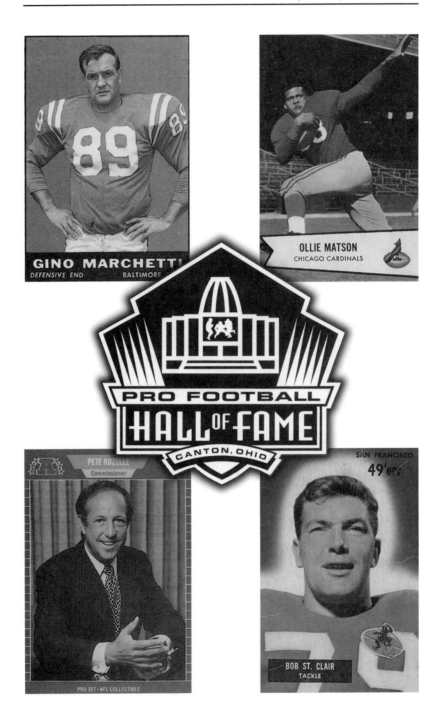

GINO MARCHETTI
DEFENSIVE END – 6' 4" 245 lbs

Pro Football Hall of Fame–
Goal Line Art, Inc. 1994

Played in the 1952 East West Shrine game with USF teammates Ollie Matson and Ed Brown. In 1969, he was selected as the best defensive end in the NFL's first 50 years. In 2000, *The Sporting News* named Gino Marchetti as the top Defensive End of the Millennium. He was drafted in the 2nd round (13th overall) by the New York Yankees in 1952. Two days after the draft, the Yanks franchise was sold back to the NFL and all assets and player were granted to the new Dallas Texans. The team folded after only one year and Marchetti's contract was assigned to Baltimore, which was busy reorganizing its club after the original Colts had folded after the 1950 season. He played in his first Pro Bowl after his first season with the Colts.

Marchetti combined size (6'4", 245) agility and amazing big-man quickness in his 13 year role as the Baltimore Colts' chief run-blocker and pass rusher. Gino was also the Colts' captain for 10 years. He became the first defensive end specialist in the early 1950's when coaches were phasing out two-way players. Gino was selected for a record of 11 straight Pro Bowls but missed one game because of an injury suffered in the 1958 NFL overtime title game against the New York Giants.

He was All-NFL seven times, missing only 1963 in the 1957-1964 span.. An all-around great defender, Marchetti is best known for his vicious pass rushing. In 1972 , his first year of eligibility, Gino was enshrined into Pro Football's Hall of Fame.

OLLIE MATSON

HALF BACK – 6' 2" 220 lbs

In 1952, Ollie starred in the East West Shrine Game along with fellow USF teammates, Gino Marchetti and Ed Brown. That same year the nation's leading rusher and scorer made Grantland Rice's *Look Magazine* All America team – as a defensive back.

At the '52 Olympics Games in Helsinki, Ollie won two medals for the United States; a bronze in the 440 meter race and a silver in the 1600 meter relay. In the 1952 NFL Draft, he was the first round (3rd overall) pick of the Chicago Cardinals. Later that year he shared Rookie of the Year honors with Hugh McElhenny of the 49ers.

After a spectacular rookie season, Ollie chose to serve his country and sit out the 1953 NFL season.

Pro Football Hall of Fame–
Goal Line Art, Inc. 1994

In 1959 Commissioner (and USF colleague) Pete Rozelle traded Matson to the Los Angeles Rams for an unheard of nine players.

Ollie was named All NFL four straight years (1954-1957) and played in five Pro Bowls. In 1956 he was chosen as Pro Bowl MVP.

He played with the following teams: 1952, 1954-1958 – Chicago Cardinals, 1959-1962 – Los Angeles Rams, 1963 – Detroit Lions, 1964-1966 – Philadelphia Eagles

Over Matson's fourteen season career he gained 12,844 combined net yards, 5,123 yards rushing, 222 receptions, 438 points, and 9 touchdowns on punt and kickoff returns. These achievements were accomplished while playing on four teams that finished above .500 for a total of two times.

In 1972, his first year of eligibility, Ollie was enshrined into Pro Football's Hall of Fame. He was presented by his former USF coach, Joe Kuharich.

Ollie Matson and Jim Thorpe share the honors of being the only Olympic Games medalists and Pro Football Hall of Fame inductees.

1952 Helsinki Olympics. Matson and members of the USA 1600-meter relay team awaiting Silver medal presentation.

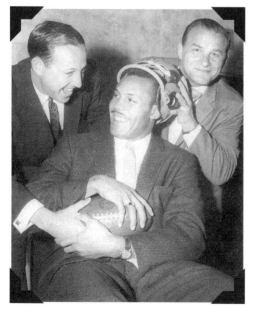

A record nine-player trade for halfback Ollie Matson! (left to right) Commissioner Pete Rozelle, Ollie Matson, and Los Angeles Rams owner, Carroll Rosenbloom.

PETE ROZELLE

NFL COMMISSIONER

Pete Rozelle graduated from USF in 1950 and became the Dons Athletic Publicist in 1951. His work at USF had come to the attention of the Los Angeles Rams and for $5500 a year, joined them as Publicity Director in 1952

In 1959 Pete engineered one of the blockbuster trades of all time in NFL history; dealing off nine players for Ollie Matson. In January of 1960, Pete was elected Commissioner of the NFL replacing Bert Bell. He presided over and watched as the league grew from 12 teams to 28 teams. From 1960 to 1962 he persuaded the teams to forgo individual TV deals for a league wide contract. Between 1963 and 1964 the NFL broadcast rights tripled to $14,000,000. Rozelle later went on to skillfully merged the NFL with

Pro Football Hall of Fame–
Goal Line Art, Inc. 1993.

the AFL; always keeping a watchful eye on the league restructuring that followed. In 1967, he presided over the first Super Bowl and turned it into a premier event. In 1970 Pete created a "national icon" - Monday Night Football. 1985 saw him become enshrined into Pro Football's Hall of Fame. Two years later, the National Football League received 2.1 billion in television rights. Pete retired as NFL Commissioner in 1989. Because of his vision and dedication to the league, the NFL continues to maintain an image of stability and integrity. In 1996 Pete Rozelle died in Rancho Santa Fe, California.

BOB ST. CLAIR

OFFENSIVE TACKLE – 6' 9" 265 lbs

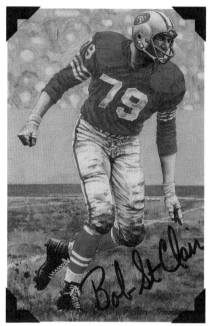

Pro Football Hall of Fame–
Goal Line Art, Inc. 1994.

Bob had completed his junior year at the University of San Francisco when it was announced that the school would disband their football program. He transferred to Tulsa at the end of the 51-52 academic year and graduated in 1953 earning All Missouri Valley Conference honors. That same year he was drafted in the 3rd round (32nd overall) by the San Francisco 49ers.

St. Clair not only had size and strength (at 6' 9" the biggest man in the NFL), but he also had speed. He excelled as a runner and pass blocker, and played equally well on goal line defense and on special teams. Bob was also the 49ers team captain for three years.

He was a starting tackle in five Pro Bowls (1957, '59, '60-'62) and an All Pro in 1955, '56, and '57. In 1956 Bob was credited with blocking ten field goal tries. He was named to first- team All-NFL three times and earned second-team births ten times, missing only 1957 because of a separated shoulder injury. In 1963 he won the Len Eshmont Award for Most Inspirational 49er.

Bob played his entire career with San Francisco. But due to a severe Achilles tendon injury, he was forced to retire from football in 1964.

In 1990 St. Clair was enshrined into Pro Football's Hall of Fame. In 1996 he was named to the 50 Year 49er All Star Team of the Decade.

On January 19, 2001 the field at Kezar Stadium, where Bob played a total of 189 games, (more than anyone else in the history of that stadium) was officially named after him. It is now Bob St. Clair Field. His honors and accolades didn't end here. On December 12, 2001 at Candlestick Park, Bob's jersey, Number 79, was retired by the San Francisco 49ers.

BURL TOLER

NATIONAL FOOTBALL LEAGUE OFFICIAL

Gino Marchetti referred to Burl Toler as "the best player on the team." Toler was drafted by the Cleveland Browns in his junior year at USF. In the 1952 All Star Game he suffered a career-ending knee injury. He never played the game again.

Upon returning to the Hilltop in 1963; Burl received his teaching credential and in 1966, his Masters Degree.

In 1965 Toler served as the first African American official in the National Football League. During those years as head linesman he worked over 500 games, including Division Playoffs, Championships and three Super Bowls including Super Bowl I.

Since 1991 he has served as an evaluator and recruiter of referees for the NFL in the western region of the United States.

National Football League Referee Burl Toler

OFFICIAL SIGNALS

MAN IN A STRIPED SHIRT

World of Sports

Art Rosenbaum
August 18, 1968

Burl Toler was the first black official in the NFL. When he was appointed in 1965, only four seasons ago, he became the lone black man operating as arbiter for any major pro sport.

Since then, Emmett Ashford was elevated to umpire in the American League (baseball), Aaron Wade was added to the list in the American Football League, and last year the National Basketball Association, with rosters of more than 50 per cent black players, named Jackie White.

This season the NFL appointed a second black line judge, Robert Beeks.

Toler does not think of himself as "another Jackie Robinson," although he concedes his presence at Kezar and other NFL parks could be considered a breakthrough.

"I have always been a competitor," he said. "I wanted to play football in the NFL but after my knee operation, competitive football was out. It was my choice to become an official, and mine only. I would not have asked for the NFL job if I did not think I was qualified. I worked high school and later college games, then I applied in 1964 to the NFL and was accepted in 1965."

"There was no race question, one way or the other. I was available, I passed the tests, I got the job. As a human being."

Burl Toler was a star center and linebacker on the University of San Francisco team that included Ollie Matson, Bob St. Clair, Gino Marchetti, Dick Stanfel, Ed Brown, Roy Barni, Mike Mergen, Red Stephens, Joe Scudero, Ralph Thomas and Merrill Peacock—every one signed by the pros.

In 1951, Joe Kuharich was the coach, and his last team was undefeated. Despite that record the economics of the game had caught up with USF and football was discontinued.

Toler was a stick out. One pro scout told The Chronicle's Darnell Wilson, "We had Burl rated with Ollie Matson as a prospect, at linebacker or center, until he crushed a knee in the Chicago All Star game." He had been signed by the Cardinals.

Linebacker and center are positions which, recent research shows, have been reserved for the white man. Toler would have broken through that barrier in 1952. He was big, fast and discerning.

Instead, he studied for his teaching credentials. He came up the chairs in San Francisco schools with a predominately black enrollment. When he was at Golden Gate school, he helped to "cool it" during the school bus fuss. Now he is vice principal at Portola Junior High. He has also served on several city appointed commissions.

"As a line judge in the NFL," said Toler, "part of my responsibility is calling pass interference. That's the call where you get a lot of help from the crowd, depending on which club you called it against. Those football fans can say some ripe things, and so can the players.

"Football players live in two different worlds. On the field they are emotionally fired up. I understand this feeling, the same that I had when I played ball. They'll say things to officials and to each other that they simply would not think of saying off the field."

The present posture and the future of the black man in America is of deep concern to Burl Toler. His role as an NFL official, in a sport watched by more people than any in America, is not inconsequential. It dramatizes the upward struggle.

It is not the answer to the struggle. The answer is..."In my school," said Toler, "we try to show the black student our respect and concern. When we show concern, he brightens. We talk to him, reason with him. That's what teaching is all about."

"It is not easy. We lose some. Good teaching, in the long run, will win for black people."

Toler is hooked on education. Man's dignity increases with knowledge.

"Our people," he said, "are becoming more and more capable of thinking for themselves. In our home we tell our own son that we, all of us, should think harder about what we want to do. Before we go off running after the shouters, we should try to learn the motives behind the movement and to consider the source."

"The activists have their rights but they say and do a lot of things I wouldn't buy. I'd be willing to bet the Olympic boycott movement fails. I like to see college youngsters weigh their own decisions, and not be led."

And then he repeated, "education will win for black people."

*   *   *

Each year the Kuharich Memorial Luncheon is held at the university where the '51 players once again have a chance to visit with their fellow teammates and coaches. Every ten years the team members and their families meet for a gala dinner celebrating USF's first and only undefeated and untied season. Their friendship has stood the test of time—and so, their legacy lives on.

10

CHAPTER TEN
1951 REVISITED

*"Id like to say thank you for your courage, thank you for being
the kinds of role models that inspire young people and inspire community.
Thank you for being who you are."*

—Dan Boggan, Senior Vice President
National Collegiate Athletic Association
50 year reunion – September 2001

San Francisco Examiner
SPORTS FINAL EDITION
Sunday, May 26, 1991

DREAM TEAM
'51 Dons, reassembling this weekend, may have been best in college football history

By: Dwight Chapin

Examiner Senior Writer

GINO MARCHETTI and Ollie Matson are two of the finest football players of all time, so their opinions on the sport should carry a little weight.

Looking back at the 1951 University of San Francisco squad on which they were teammates, Marchetti said:

"If this team had played at Notre Dame, they'd still be writing books about it."

1951 USF Dons, May 25, 1991 - 40 Year Reunion

Shown here recreating their team photo in the 1952 USF Yearbook are: First Row: left to right: Greg Hillig, Vince Tringali, Hal Sachs, Lou Stephens, USF President Rev. John Lo Schiavo, S.J., who as a young scholastic was freshman barracks prefect in 1951; Ralph Thomas, Merrill Peacock, Bill Henneberry, Jim Kearney. Second Row: Jim Whitney, Joe Scudero, Ollie Matson, former NFL Commissioner Pete Rozelle, who was Athletic News Director in '51; Gino Marchetti, Burl Toler, Vince Sakowski, Roy Giorgi, Bob St. Clair. Third Row: Dick Huxley, Bob Shaeffer, John Dwyer, Larry Slajchert, Jim Madden, Tom Montero, Tim Moriarity, Bob Springer, Joe Arenivar. Back Row: Ed Dawson, Dick Arnoldy, Bill Dando, Walt Roland, Jack Becker, Dick Columbini, Roy Bruna, Team Manager Dick Domeno. - Photo by George Krause

Matson went a step further. "I think you could have taken that team into the pros and within a couple of years it would have won the league championship," he said. "I really believe that. We had some great ballplayers."

No one would argue that point. The '51 Dons are the only college team ever to have three members (halfback Matson and linemen Marchetti and Bob St. Clair) inducted into the Pro Football Hall of Fame. And that doesn't count Pete Rozelle, who made a slightly larger name for himself in his 29 years as NFL commissioner than as USF's 25 year old athletic publicist four decades ago.

It doesn't stop there.

Bob St. Clair's induction into Pro Football's Hall of Fame, 1990.

Five more players from that magnificent team, quarterback Ed Brown, halfback Joe "Scooter" Scudero and linemen Lou Stephens, Ralph Thomas and Mike Mergen, played in the NFL. Lineman Burl Toler, who Marchetti still believes was the Dons' best player, undoubtedly would have, too, if he hadn't torn up a knee in the 1951 College All Star Game and had to quit playing. But Toler was in the NFL far longer than any of his teammates, serving 25 years as one of the league's best officials.

And coach Joe Kuharich went on to be an 11 year head coach in the pros, with the Chicago Cardinals, Washington Redskins and Philadelphia Eagles, albeit without the same success he enjoyed in that one shining season at USF.

Kuharich and a handful of others from the '51 Dons are gone now, but 33 of the 39 alumni returned to San Francisco this weekend for a 40 year reunion of what just might have been the best college football team ever. Or at least The Best Team Almost Nobody Ever Heard Of.

For many of those long-ago Dons, 1951 was a beginning, a springboard to athletic fame, productive and rewarding careers and, in most cases, exemplary lives.

For USF, it was an ending - the last year of big time intercollegiate football at the school before the sport was dropped because of mounting financial problems.

The season ended in frustration both on and off the field.

"Unbeaten, untied and uninvited," a San Francisco newspaperman wrote, and that proved to be a lasting epitaph.

The '51 Dons won all nine of their games, becoming the only team in school history to go undefeated. That was supposed to be good enough to earn them a berth in a major bowl game - the Orange Bowl was most prominently mentioned.

The Dons beat Loyola University in Los Angeles in their final regular season game, and the mood on the train ride home was nothing short of euphoric. When the squad arrived in San Francisco, however, the joy quickly vanished. The players got the news that Georgia Tech and Baylor had been picked for the Orange Bowl. The other bowls ignored USF, too, even the Sun Bowl, which selected College of the Pacific, a team the Dons had beaten soundly during the season.

A Soft Schedule

The official explanation for the Orange Bowl snub of the Dons was this: "The selection committee felt that USF's schedule was in no way comparable to that played by Georgia Tech," chairman Van Kussrow said. "We felt we had to get a team which the public would consider a match for Georgia Tech."

USF's schedule undeniably was soft. It included two service teams, the

Camp Pendleton Marines and the San Diego Naval Training Center, San Jose State (twice), Idaho, Fordham, Santa Clara, UOP and Loyola.

The lack of name opponents such as California, Stanford and USC was not too hard to figure.

"We tried to get teams like that to play us," Rozelle remembered, "but they wouldn't, because they saw no merit in possibly losing to us."

Many felt the Orange Bowl rejection had as much to do with prevailing racial attitudes as quality of opponents.

Two of the Dons' stars, Matson and Toler, were, in the accepted terminology of the time, "Negroes." And San Francisco sportscaster Ira Blue reported that he had been told the Orange, Sugar and Gator bowls all declined to invite teams with "Negro" players.

Scudero since has suggested that USF should have sent Matson and Toler to a bowl game and left the rest of the team home, because those two could match anyone else's 22.

Matson has a milder reaction now to what may have been a racially motivated decision.

"The situation was so different at that time," he said. "You have to face reality."

Just as real was the money USF lost by not going to a bowl, money that might have saved the football program for another season and kept players such as St. Clair from having to transfer to complete their college athletic eligibility.

Because of circumstance, the Dons of '51 were forced to begin living with memories a little sooner than many of their contemporaries. The recollections remain fresh and sharp, probably because the players still care a great deal about each other.

"We've always had a unique closeness," said backup quarterback Bill Henneberry. "This weekend may be the first time we've gotten everybody together since '51, but we still meet, still communicate, still share a lot."

"Forty years ago, we formed lifelong relationships," said Toler. "We're still like family."

St. Clair believes the reason the players had such rapport right from the start was most of them were local products. "We had a Bay Area pride," he said.

And the togetherness was reinforced by the fact that players and staff members such as Rozelle lived together in old ROTC barracks on campus.

Lynn's Keen Eye For Talent

The team mainly was put together not by Kuharich, who found recruiting anathema, but by assistant coach Brad Lynn, who uncovered prospects in some unlikely locations. He found Marchetti, a World War ll veteran, tending bar in Antioch, for example.

But Lynn had a keen eye for talent, particularly talent other people had missed, and Kuharich was a master at molding it.

Kuharich's players feared him while they revered him. He was a mild mannered, almost shy man away from football, but things changed dramatically on the practice field.

"We nicknamed him "The Barracuda," St. Clair said. "He came from the old school of hard-nosed Notre Dame football. In the pre-season, he took us to train in Corning, up near Red Bluff. It was about 120 degrees up there, and he wouldn't let us drink water. He'd put flakes of oatmeal in the water buckets so we couldn't swallow it. We'd just have to rinse it around in our mouths and spit it out."

Kuharich also came up with something called "The Pits," a torture drill in which the coach would test his players against each other one-on-one, within the confines of a couple of narrowly spaced posts.

"There was no going around somebody in "The Pits." said lineman Vince Tringali. "You had to go through him. I used to avoid the big guys like St. Clair and Marchetti. But the small guys like Thomas and Greg Hillig were crazy, too."

In Top Physical Shape

Kuharich had plenty of method in his seeming madness.

"Joe knew that about 15 of us would play all the games on both offense and defense, so he wanted us to be in top physical condition," said St. Clair. "We sure were. We were like caged animals."

The feeling has passed but not the remembrance.

"I think if you asked the players on that '51 team what they got out of playing for USF, to a man they'd say everything else they ever did in life was easy," Tringali said.

"Kuharich had an aura about him that was unbelievable. I always felt like playing for him was a matter of survival. I was never that great a player, but I worked very hard. Fortunately, you didn't have to be the best player with Joe, because he rewarded hard work."

Fordham Game A Highlight

Hard work and a high degree of skill led to some never-to-be equaled results.

The highlight of the '51 season may have been a late October trip to New York, where USF played Fordham. Rozelle, in particular, was nervous about that game because he'd been trying to convince the nations press how good the Dons were and was heavily promoting star halfback Matson for All American in the process.

Rozelle flirted with heart failure as Matson dropped the opening kickoff, but Ollie then picked up the ball and went 94 yards for a touchdown, the first of three as he gained 302 yards rushing and returning kicks.

Rozelle was relieved; Matson's teammates were enthralled. "When he went by us on that first touchdown," Tringali said, "Marchetti said he was sure glad Ollie was on our team. I said I was, too."

USF was hard-pressed to win that game, 32-26, but most of the season was a good deal easier going for the Dons, Rozelle gratefully included.

"By the fourth quarter of most of our games at Kezar Stadium," Rozelle said, "we were so far ahead, the band was playing our theme song, *Good Night, Irene.*"

The associations made in that magical season on The Hilltop - "A very happy, uncomplicated period of time," Rozelle said - were never forgotten.

Bonds Stayed Intact

When he coached in the NFL and Notre Dame, Kuharich, who died in 1981, frequently employed his USF proteges as players and assistant coaches. They extended the bond. As general manager of the Rams, Rozelle traded nine players to the Cardinals for Matson. As NFL commissioner, Rozelle hired Kuharich as supervisor of officials and signed Burl Toler as the league's first black official.

The camaraderie was still so thick you could cut it during all the reminiscing this weekend.

So was the pride of men who as a group may have been largely ignored by football historians but are well aware of what they accomplished.

Said Henneberry, "I think what our team did and what our players have gone on to do in life indicates that we probably were as modestly good as we thought we were."

*   *   *

The Times-Picayune

New Orleans, Louisiana

JANUARY 29, 1994

51 Dons Deserved Better Fate

By: Peter Finney, columnist

Before the San Francisco 49ers came the San Francisco Dons.

Before Joe Montana and Company, there was Ollie Matson and Company, and what company it was.

Before the procession of Vince Lombardi trophies into the 49ers' trophy case, there was no trophy for the University of San Francisco, only memories of what might have been, making it sort of a Camelot-like wisp of glory.

Magical and frustrating, it was a history lesson Bill Kuharich, the Saints' director of player personnel, learned at home growing up. It was a verbal history passed on by his dad, whose favorite pastime was reliving the football season of 1951.

So it's understandable the name San Francisco stirs mixed feelings in Bill Kuharich. While one San Francisco, the one in the Superdome tonight, has made life miserable for the Saints, the San Francisco he never knew was a delightful storybook.

Two years before Bill was born, Joe Kuharich coached the '51 Dons to a 9-0 record. By the time Bill became old enough to absorb history, he was convinced the '51 Dons were the greatest college team of all time.

His dad told him.

"Son," said father to son, "if that team had Notre Dame on their jerseys, they would have built a monument in their memory."

Joe Kuharich knew all about Fighting Irish mystique. He was born in South Bend, Ind. He played for the Irish. He coached the Irish. But there never was a doubt in the mind of Joe Kuharich the best college team ever was his unbeaten, untied and unnoticed Dons of '51.

Here are the facts: The '51 Dons sent 10 players to the NFL, including three - Ollie Matson, Gino Marchetti, Bob St. Clair - who wound up in the Pro Football Hall of Fame. No other college team can make that statement.

Nor did any other college team's PR director go on to become NFL commissioner and a Hall of Famer, which is what happened to Pete Rozelle.

Still, despite Matson's heroics and Rozelle's pulling the publicity strings, fate was cruel.

Because of their schedule, the Dons were ranked 14th in the final Associated Press poll. It wasn't their fault. The West Coast powers at that time, Cal and Stanford, refused to play them. After breezing to nine straight victories, they awaited an invitation to the Orange Bowl but were passed over. The dons thought an invitation to the Sun Bowl might be in the works, but that went instead to College of Pacific, a team the Dons crushed, 47-14.

And that wasn't all.

Matson, an Olympic sprinter who led the country in rushing and points scored, made the All American team, almost as an afterthought, as a defensive back.

But there was no room on the team for the two other future Hall of Famers, not for Marchetti, who would be voted the NFL's top defensive end for the first 50 years, not for St. Clair, a five time Pro Bowler.

It was no secret why the Dons were shunned by the bowls. It wasn't schedule. It was *racial*. Matson was black, as was Burl Toler, an outstanding linebacker whose pro career was short-circuited by a knee injury suffered in the College All Star game.

"My dad always felt, if he had gotten the chance to play in the pros, Burl Toler was good enough to get into the Hall of Fame," Kuharich said. "It really was an amazing story. It was pretty much of a home-grown team. Matson, Marchetti and St. Clair were from the San Francisco area. So were most of the other players. Still, while the home crowds were loyal, they were small."

The Jesuit school was losing $70,000 a year on football. When a bowl invitation did not materialize after the '51 season, the football program was discontinued. It wouldn't be long before USF, featuring a guy named Bill Russell, would be celebrating basketball championships.

But the football memories remain. A Joe Kuharich memorial Scholarship, awarded annually to a student-athlete in a varsity sport, was inaugurated last year.

In 1970, Joe Kuharich, who had gone on to coach the Cardinals, the Redskins and the Eagles, was told he had bone cancer and had two years to live. For 11 years, he fought the good fight.

He fought it talking football, mostly about the '51 Dons.

"He convinced me," said Bill Kuharich 43 years later. "The '51 Dons were the best college team of all time."

*   *   *

1951 USF Dons, 50 Year Reunion - September 29, 2001

Row 1: (left to right) Bill Henneberry, Dick Huxley, Joe Scudero, Vince Sakowski, Jim Whitney, Vince Tringali, Jim Madden, Bob Schaeffer, Roy Bruna. Row 2: (left to right) Ralph Thomas, Dick colombini, Roy Giorgi, Tom Montero, Bob Weibel, John Dwyer, Lou Stephens, Row 3: (left to right) Burl Toler, Hal Sachs, Dick Domeno, Gene De Martini, Bob St. Clair, Dick Arnoldy, Ed Dawson, Larry Slajchert

The New York Times

September 23, 2001

Once Uninvited, Undefeated and Unsung, but No Longer Unappreciated

By: Dave Anderson

It wouldn't happen now. If a college football team had a 9-0 season with a breakaway halfback who led the nation in rushing and was a world-class runner, a lineman who had been a battlefield Army veteran and an end who ate raw steak—not rare, raw—it would soar in the polls, inspire television highlights and create a swarm of bowl-game invitations.

Oh, and the starters also played both offense and defense.

But this happened 50 years ago, not today. The 1951 University of San Francisco Dons were not only undefeated and untied but also uninvited and unsung, a forgotten 14th in the final Associated Press poll. Because two of their best players were black, Ollie Matson and Burl Toler, they were ignored by Southern-based bowl committees of that era.

Joe Kuharich, the coach who would go on to Notre Dame and three pro teams, had told the dons that the Orange Bowl was considering them.

"Joe later went around asking guys if they would go to a bowl game without Burl or me," Matson, the breakaway back, recalled from his Los Angeles home. "But Gino Marchetti said, 'No, we ain't gonna go without Burl and Ollie.' "

That year's Orange, Sugar and Gator Bowl committees were later reported to have disregarded any teams with black players.

"It wasn't just me," Marchetti said from his home in West Chester, Pa. "The whole team didn't want to go if Burl and Ollie couldn't go."

Marchetti, who at 17 had fought in the Battle of the Bulge during World War II, was the leader of the Dons, just as an All-Pro defensive end he later was the leader of the Baltimore Colts that won the 1958 and 1959 National Football League championships.

"Burl Toler was our best all-around player," Marchetti said. "But after Burl hurt his right knee in the College All-Star Game, he never played again. For a tall guy, he was the best tackler I've ever seen. He would've been a great outside linebacker in the NFL."

"I was in the hospital for 30 days with torn ligaments," Toler said. "When I got out, the doctor told me, 'You have a good knee, but if you get hurt again, I might not be able to fix it that well again.'"

Marchetti, Matson and Bob St. Clair, the raw-meat eater, who evolved into a 49ers offensive tackle, represent the only college team with three players in the Pro Football Hall of Fame.

"When those three guys excelled and five others made it to the NFL," said Bill Henneberry, the backup quarterback, "We realized maybe we were a good as we thought we were."

Henneberry, now the USF director of athletic development, has organized a 50th reunion of the 1951 Dons next Saturday night at the Westin St. Francis Hotel in San Francisco.

"We're supposed to visit the White House to get an apology for the way the bowls snubbed us," Henneberry said. "About three weeks ago, the White House told us they were having trouble clearing the President's calendar, that maybe it would happen in October. But ever since the terrorist attacks, we understandably have not heard anything."

Ed Brown, the Dons' quarterback, went on to the NFL, as did halfback Joe (Scooter) Scudero, guard Louis (Red) Stephens, tackle Mike Mergen and end Ralph Thomas.

Another member of that group also went to the NFL – the Dons' "athletic-news director," a USF graduate named Pete Rozelle, the Los Angeles Rams' general manager who traded nine players to acquire Matson from the Cardinals before he was elected commissioner in 1960.

"When we played Fordham at Downing Stadium in Randalls Island in '51," Matson said, "Pete told me, 'If you don't play well in New York, you can forget about making All-America.'"

Against Fordham, then a respected major college team, Matson returned two kickoffs 94 and 90 yards for touchdowns in a 32-26 victory as the Marchetti-led defense held the Rams to 61 rushing yards. In a season when tailback Dick Kazmaier of Princeton was voted the Heisman Trophy and tailback Hank Lauricella led Tennessee to the No. 1 ranking, Grantland Rice did put Matson on his All-America team, as a defensive back.

The next year, Matson, running for the United States in the 1952 Olympics at Helsinki, earned a bronze medal in the 400-meter run and a silver medal in the 4x400 relay.

Most critics devalued the Dons because of a schedule that included San Jose State twice, Idaho and two service teams, San Diego Naval and the Pendleton (Calif.) Marines.

"Our problem was that teams like Stanford and Cal knew how good we were but there was no advantage for them in playing us," Marchetti said. "The best team we played was College of the Pacific with Eddie LeBaron, and we won, 47-14. But they went to the Sun Bowl and we didn't go anywhere."

Without a bowl-game check to offset a $70,000 loss, the Jesuit administrators at USF dropped football.

"But if our 1951 team had been at Notre Dame," said Marchetti, "they would still be writing books about us."

*   *   *

Throughout the evening of the fifty year celebration, there were many guest speakers who praised the decision surrounding that storybook season. Four of those esteemed guest speakers had this to say about that unprecedented season:

"When you think about the time the decision was made by the Dons not to play in the bowl…it warms my heart and gives me hope that we as people will continue to learn that standing together we are stronger. That's the American spirit."

—Dan Boggan, Senior Vice President
National Collegiate Athletic Association

"These men exemplified the values that remain at the core of our identity as a Jesuit Catholic university," USF President Stephen A. Privett, S.J. said at the dinner. "I refer to dedication to a common good, rather than the interests of any one individual, respect for the dignity and worth of every human being, and an unwavering commitment to excellence on the field, in the classroom, and in their personal and professional lives. The men who we celebrate this evening paid a price for their integrity. They refused a bowl bid rather than compromise their values. They sacrificed glory for honor and character."

*   *   *

On this same topic San Francisco Mayor Willie Brown was quoted as saying, "It may very well be the most outstanding athletic decision ever made by a university. They were way ahead of their time…and it truly was a monumentally important decision."

*   *   *

Guard Vince Tringali summed up the players' feelings, "The spirit of this team is infinite. It never stops, it's always with us. These were the most loyal guys I ever played with, and the most loyal men I ever met."

*   *   *

The story of the 1951 Dons does not end here.

In the year 2000, I contacted Senator Barbara Boxer and Congressman Steve Largent to tell them about this unique group of men, and the unselfish decision they had made, as a team, almost fifty years ago.

I requested that this '51 USF squad be honored and recognized by the President of the United States, at the White House, for the courage they portrayed on as well as off the football field. What you are about to read in this next chapter is something no other college team in the nation has ever achieved.

11

CHAPTER ELEVEN
The Road to the White House

"Now, therefore, be it Resolved, That the Senate applauds the undefeated and untied 1951 University of San Francisco Dons football team for its determination, commitment and integrity both on and off the playing field; and acknowledges that the treatment endured by this team was wrong and that recognition for its accomplishments is long over due."

—Senator Barbara Boxer
Senate Resolution 346
July 27, 2000

NOTE: At this time we are waiting to hear from the White House as to when the 1951 team will be recognized and honored by the President. The time frame will depend upon the activities that are in progress since the attacks of September 11. Senators Barbara Boxer and Dianne Feinstein, Congressman Steve Largent, and Congresswoman Lynn Woolsey are all in support of this momentous occasion.

$\mathfrak{San}$ $\mathfrak{Francisco}$ $\mathfrak{Chronicle}$

SATURDAY, JULY 8, 2000

GIVING '51 DONS THEIR DUE

Presidential apology asked to atone for racist snub that kept greatest USF football team from bowl games

By: Ken Garcia

This country has slowly come to grips with many of the past cultural and social mistakes made on issues of race and color. And now an opportunity has arisen to correct one for the green and gold - the favored hues of the USF Dons.

It's been almost 50 years since one of the greatest snubs in the history of collegiate sports took place; one that can never be changed but could finally be addressed. It's a matter now before President Clinton, and one that - if he makes the right call and issues a long overdue apology -will show the rest of the nation why San Francisco has always been ahead of its time in matters of equality and acceptance

Not to mention being one of the great sports capitals of the past century, no matter the key omissions.

And there is none larger than the fate of the 1951 USF football team, a juggernaut that the record books show went unbeaten, untied, and unbelievably unrecognized. A team that would, by almost any comparison, be considered one of the finest gridiron groups ever assembled. Yet one that has been remembered by sports historians as the best team no one ever heard of, at least outside the Bay Area.

The 1951 Dons are now best remembered not in the collegiate ranks, but in the larger sphere of the National Football League. And that is because nine - if not for injury it would have been ten - of their starters went directly to the NFL. There is no way to compare that with other college football powers, because no school has ever come close.

And then it gets really ridiculous.

Five of those nine players went on to play in the NFL Pro Bowl. And three of those five - Bob St. Clair, Ollie Matson and Gino Marchetti - have been inducted into the Pro Hall of Fame, the most ever from a single team.

And perhaps the most amazing part of it is that while major powers like Alabama and Michigan drew blue-chip athletes from around the country to play for their universities, USF in 1951 was a tiny Jesuit hilltop school with an all male enrollment of 1,276 students that managed to lure one player from San Luis Obispo. A good basketball school that with the addition of Bill Russell and K.C. Jones a few years later, would become known as a great basketball school.

But for one shining season, USF's football team stood alone, though the record book will show otherwise. It will also indicate that Georgia Tech and Baylor played in the Orange Bowl, that the University of the Pacific, thrashed by the Dons, played in the Sun Bowl and that the Sugar Bowl and the Gator Bowl invited other teams, teams that had been beaten, but teams that were more acceptable to a Southern audience.

In other words, teams that did not have "Negro" players. And the Dons had two, two of the finest athletes to ever emerge from the Bay Area: Matson and Burl Toler.

The team learned that one bowl game was interested in inviting them - but only if they agreed to leave their two black players at home. But the Dons, a close group even to this day, adamantly refused. Which is why Sports Illustrated's Ron Fimrite wrote that the 1951 team "was ignored by history, never mentioned among the legends - the Four Horsemen, the Seven Blocks of Granite, Mr. Inside and Mr. Outside....(though) it is possible that there never was a better college football team."

Forty nine years later there is a movement afoot to finally give the team its long overdue national recognition. At the urging of author Kristine Clark, who is penning a book about the unsung team, Senator Barbara Boxer has written a letter to the president asking him to correct a long-standing injustice.

"The Dons were a gifted team that for the most objectionable of reasons missed out on a once-in-a-lifetime chance to prove themselves before a national audience," Boxer wrote. "Now, almost 50 years later, it is entirely appropriate for these athletes to receive the attention and accolades they earned but were denied."

Reached yesterday by telephone, Boxer described the event as a "sad and painful incident" that deserves national attention." We can't undo the hurt and the harm of deed, but the fact is you can say you're sorry, especially to those two players," she said. "I think the fact that the rest of the team refused to go is an act of heroism."

Matson said it was a major disappointment to the team that it wasn't invited to a bowl, and being named first team All American for leading the nation in rushing that year was small consolation, especially since, in a most curious vote, he made the team as a defensive back.

"The truth is, how could you not think about it," he told me the other day. "Obviously, we were aware that we had two black players, but it never occurred to me until we didn't get invited that we wouldn't be going to a bowl game. As the years go by, it may not mean as much, but it would be nice if the team could be honored in some way."

Racism may have stopped the Dons from being nationally recognized, but it certainly never stopped Matson and Toler from moving on to superlative careers. In 1952, Matson won two medals at the Olympic Games in Helsinki and then went to spend 14 years in the NFL, gaining nearly 13,000 all purpose yards. Upon his retirement from the game, he coached and taught in Los Angeles public schools, and spent 10 years working as the event supervisor for the Los Angeles Coliseum.

Toler, who many scouts considered the best athlete on the USF team, suffered a severe knee injury in the 1952 College All Star Game, was drafted by the Cleveland Browns but never reported after his operation. He ended up going back to USF to get his master's degree in educational administration, became the first black secondary school principal in the city's history and later became director of services for the San Francisco Community College District.

And, in one respect, he had the longest NFL career of any of his heralded teammates, since he spent 25 years as a highly respected NFL referee.

St. Clair, who played 11 years with the 49ers as a 6 foot 9, 265 pound tackle was considered one of the finest linemen of his day, said it was a bitter disappointment for the great USF team, because after two seasons together, they realized how good they had become.

"Nobody wanted to play us after the 1950 season because they realized it was a lose-lose situation for the big schools," he said. "Here was this tiny Jesuit school from San Francisco beating up everybody. So the race thing was just another reason for someone not to invite us, because we were just very good, and nobody from our team even thought about black and white. But times were different them".

There was one other notable feature about that great '51 team. It was also the school's last.

USF's football program had been losing about $70,000 a year, a financial hit that the Jesuits could no longer afford. So after the team declined to play in a Southern bowl game without Toler and Matson, USF President Rev. William J. Dunne sadly announced that the school was dropping football.

Toler said it would be a nice gesture if President Clinton takes Boxer's suggestion and invites the team to the White House to praise the team for its accomplishments and apologize for the slight. But ever the gentleman,

Toler said he harbors no hard feelings toward the bowl game officials who denied the team its just due.

"It was always my attitude in life that I can deal with anything that comes my way," he said. "I always try to keep moving forward, and not look back. Going to the White House would be a nice gesture, and a welcome one, but it means just as much to me today that my teammates agreed not to play without Ollie and me."

*   *   *

Marin Independent Journal

April 10, 2001	TUESDAY	Marin County, California

Overdue honor for '51 Dons

Novato woman works to get USF champs to White House

By: Dave Albee
   I.J. reporter

Kris Clark of Novato has written a book about the undefeated, untied and under-appreciated 1951 University of San Francisco football team. She has sent it to a publisher, but she is taking the story all the way to the commander-in-chief.

Inspired by Clark's passion in the project, U.S. Sen. Barbara Boxer of Greenbrae, D-Calif., has written to President George W. Bush requesting that the '51 USF team - denied an invitation to play Georgia Tech in the Orange Bowl because it had two black players - be invited to the White House 50 years after the fact.

Clark, who has been contacted by the White House, has provided information on the team so it can be honored by the president, possibly in June.

"I want this to happen," Clark said yesterday.

"With Kris doing this, its almost 90 percent sure," said Pro Football Hall of Fame member Bob St. Clair, a Santa Rosa resident who was an end on that USF team. "She's a bulldog. She's so persistent. I think that's part of her charm."

Clark's quest for the White House invitation started four years ago when she found an anonymous videotape left on her desk at USF, where she was working on her doctorate in education. To this day, she does not know where the tape came from or who passed it to her, but she didn't drop the ball once she saw what was on it.

That night, Clark and her husband, Bill, watched a seven minute presentation by NFL Films about the '51 USF team that went 9-0 and ended its season with a convincing 42-14 win in Stockton over a previously unbeaten College of the Pacific.

The Dons had the best team on the West Coast, but Southeast Conference officials blocked an invitation for them to play unbeaten Georgia Tech in the Orange Bowl - unless the Dons chose to play without fullback Ollie Matson and standout lineman Burl Toler, who were black.

"That's ridiculous," St. Clair said. "We didn't even vote under such a stupid request."

So the Dons stayed home and the football program disbanded the next year because of financial problems.

"What people didn't realize is because a team didn't go to a bowl, it ended the football program - we just couldn't afford it," USF executive athletic director Bill Hogan said. "Going to a bowl game would have provided USF a way to maintain the program. The decision by the USF team was courageous. If they had done something different, they would've had the big payday, so to speak. That is something that should be admired."

Ten players - including Matson and Toler - were drafted into the NFL. Four members of that '51 team - St. Clair, Matson, Gino Marchetti and team public relations director, Pete Rozelle, who eventually because NFL commissioner - were inducted into the Pro Football Hall of Fame.

Still, as NFL Films president Steve Sabol said on the tape, the team is "just a footnote. The best team you never heard of."

The Clarks decided to do something to change that.

Kris Clark was so moved that, with the support of USF director of athletic development Bill Henneberry, she traveled coast to coast to interview subjects for her book, titled "Undefeated, Untied, and Uninvited." She met with Marchetti and Madelyn Kuharich, wife of deceased USF coach Joe Kuharich, in Pennsylvania, tackle Lou Stephens in Albuquerque, end Ralph Thomas in Reno, and with Matson in Los Angeles. She interviewed more than a dozen team members.

The more Clark spoke with them, the more she realized the disappointment they felt about being a championship team without a bowl bid. They outscored their opponents by an average of 33-8 and whipped Tulsa, the nation's No. 1 ranked offensive team, which had been a heavy favorite to beat the Dons.

The only opponent they could not beat that year was discrimination.

"The way these guys were treated wasn't right," Bill Clark told his wife. "Something ought to be done."

Bill suggested taking the cause to the top; the White House.

Kris started contacting her elected officials, including Boxer. She befriended St. Clair, 41 years after her dad first took her to see him play for the 49ers at Kezar Stadium. She left her job as assistant principal at Del Mar Middle School in Tiburon to teach physical education at Galileo High School in the city so she could devote more time to write her book.

"As time went on, this thing started ballooning up," St. Clair said. "She's talking to Barbara Boxer...It just mushroomed."

Clark's determination paid off.

Boxer, in a letter dated June 22, 2000, urged President Clinton to honor the '51 USF team. Soon after, Boxer's political friends joined her.

In a letter on July 27, 2000 Sen. Dianne Feinstein, D-Calif. asked President Clinton to stage a ceremony for the Dons at the White House.

That same day, Boxer submitted a resolution in the U.S. Senate that the '51 team be given a tribute at the White House. It passed unanimously. She followed that up with another letter, dated Nov. 30, 2000, insisting the president invite the Dons to the White House before the close of his administration.

In a letter on August 18, 2000, Rep. Lynn Woolsey, D-Petaluma, also asked Clinton to stage a ceremony for the Dons.

Finally, former Seattle Seahawks' wide receiver Steve Largent, now a member of the U.S. House of Representatives, took up the cause. Largent is a member of the Pro Football Hall of Fame and the University of Tulsa Hall of Fame. In a letter dated March 20 of this year, the republican from Oklahoma asked Bush to pick up the ball.

St. Clair was invited to the White House 10 years ago by Bush's father after the former 49ers' All Pro lineman was elected to the Pro Football Hall of Fame. Today he's eager for a return engagement with the '51 team.

"I just think it's a great accolade for us. I'd be thrilled to death," St. Clair said. "And naturally being a Republican, I'd be more thrilled."

So would Kris Clark, who would attend such a ceremony at the White House to honor a team that played when she was only a year old.

"It's my time," Clark said.

It's her story, too, and she's sticking to it.

*   *   *

BARBARA BOXER
CALIFORNIA

COMMITTEES:
BUDGET
ENVIRONMENT
AND PUBLIC WORKS
FOREIGN RELATIONS

United States Senate

HART SENATE OFFICE BUILDING
SUITE 112
WASHINGTON, DC 20510-0505
(202) 224-3553
senator@boxer.senate.gov
http://boxer.senate.gov

August 7, 2000

The President
The White House
Washington, DC 20500

Dear Mr. President:

Please find the enclosed Senate Resolution (S.Res. 346) that I introduced honoring the 1951 University of San Francisco Dons football team. This resolution passed on July 27.

Since my letter of June 22 requesting that you consider inviting the team to the White House, there has been a considerable amount of media and other interest in the 1951 Dons story of courage in the face of injustice.

As I related in my earlier letter, the Dons went undefeated and untied in 1951. But despite the fact that some consider them to have been one of the greatest college football squads ever, these deserving athletes were denied the chance to compete in a bowl game because two of the team's players were African-American.

There is growing support in the Bay Area and beyond to honor the 1951 Dons. The team is remarkable for its achievements on the football field, but also for the players' decision to stand together in the face of bigotry and, as a consequence, forego the chance of a lifetime.

Now, almost 50 years later, I believe it is wholly appropriate that the Dons be afforded the opportunity they were once denied to gather as a team on the national stage. Their talent and heroism has the power to touch people across the country. Your inviting them to the White House would be a most fitting tribute to an exceptional group of athletes and individuals.

Sincerely,

Barbara Boxer
United States Senator

BB/jo
enclosure

| 1700 MONTGOMERY STREET SUITE 240 SAN FRANCISCO, CA 94111 (415) 403-0100 | 312 N. SPRING STREET SUITE 1748 LOS ANGELES, CA 90012 (213) 894-5000 | 501 'I' STREET SUITE 7-600 SACRAMENTO, CA 95814 (916) 448-2787 | 1130 'O' STREET SUITE 2450 FRESNO, CA 93721 (559) 497-5109 | 600 'B' STREET SUITE 2240 SAN DIEGO, CA 92101 (619) 239-3884 | 201 NORTH 'E' STREET SUITE 210 SAN BERNARDINO, CA 92401 (909) 888-8525 |

Letter to President from Senator Barbara Boxer

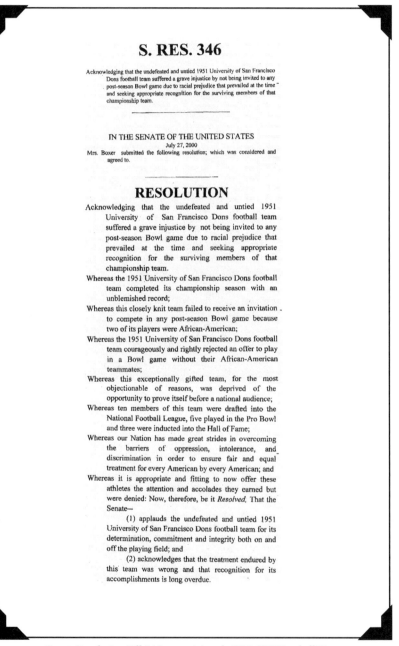

S. RES. 346

Acknowledging that the undefeated and untied 1951 University of San Francisco Dons football team suffered a grave injustice by not being invited to any post-season Bowl game due to racial prejudice that prevailed at the time and seeking appropriate recognition for the surviving members of that championship team.

IN THE SENATE OF THE UNITED STATES
July 27, 2000
Mrs. Boxer submitted the following resolution; which was considered and agreed to.

RESOLUTION

Acknowledging that the undefeated and untied 1951 University of San Francisco Dons football team suffered a grave injustice by not being invited to any post-season Bowl game due to racial prejudice that prevailed at the time and seeking appropriate recognition for the surviving members of that championship team.

Whereas the 1951 University of San Francisco Dons football team completed its championship season with an unblemished record;

Whereas this closely knit team failed to receive an invitation to compete in any post-season Bowl game because two of its players were African-American;

Whereas the 1951 University of San Francisco Dons football team courageously and rightly rejected an offer to play in a Bowl game without their African-American teammates;

Whereas this exceptionally gifted team, for the most objectionable of reasons, was deprived of the opportunity to prove itself before a national audience;

Whereas ten members of this team were drafted into the National Football League, five played in the Pro Bowl and three were inducted into the Hall of Fame;

Whereas our Nation has made great strides in overcoming the barriers of oppression, intolerance, and discrimination in order to ensure fair and equal treatment for every American by every American; and

Whereas it is appropriate and fitting to now offer these athletes the attention and accolades they earned but were denied: Now, therefore, be it *Resolved,* That the Senate—

(1) applauds the undefeated and untied 1951 University of San Francisco Dons football team for its determination, commitment and integrity both on and off the playing field; and

(2) acknowledges that the treatment endured by this team was wrong and that recognition for its accomplishments is long overdue.

Senate Resolution Bill 346 recognizing the 1951 USF Football Team

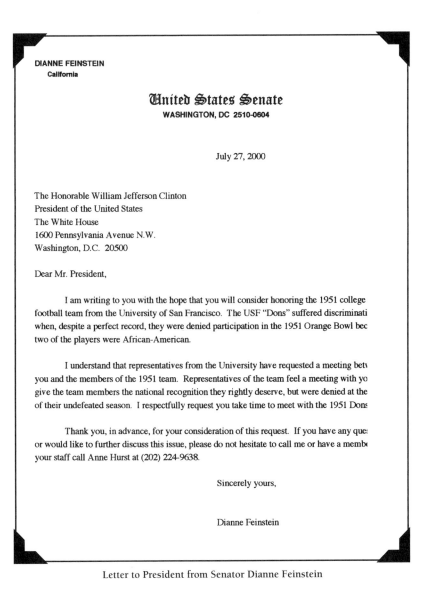

DIANNE FEINSTEIN
California

United States Senate
WASHINGTON, DC 2510-0604

July 27, 2000

The Honorable William Jefferson Clinton
President of the United States
The White House
1600 Pennsylvania Avenue N.W.
Washington, D.C. 20500

Dear Mr. President,

I am writing to you with the hope that you will consider honoring the 1951 college football team from the University of San Francisco. The USF "Dons" suffered discriminati when, despite a perfect record, they were denied participation in the 1951 Orange Bowl bec two of the players were African-American.

I understand that representatives from the University have requested a meeting betv you and the members of the 1951 team. Representatives of the team feel a meeting with yo give the team members the national recognition they rightly deserve, but were denied at the of their undefeated season. I respectfully request you take time to meet with the 1951 Dons

Thank you, in advance, for your consideration of this request. If you have any que: or would like to further discuss this issue, please do not hesitate to call me or have a memb your staff call Anne Hurst at (202) 224-9638.

Sincerely yours,

Dianne Feinstein

Letter to President from Senator Dianne Feinstein

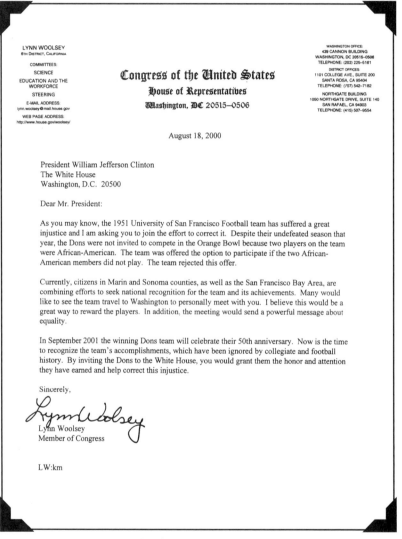

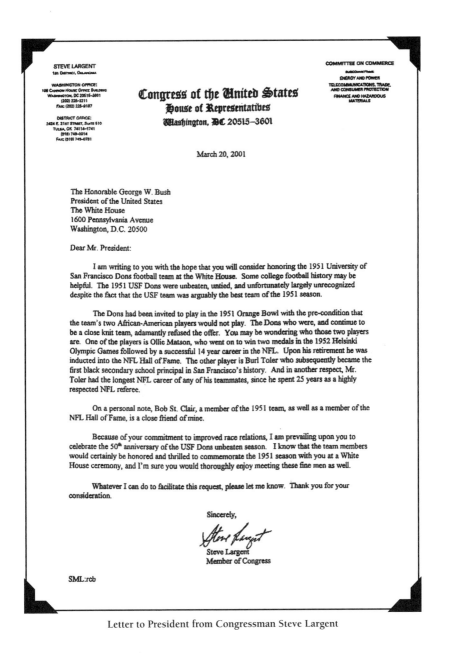

STEVE LARGENT
1st District, Oklahoma

WASHINGTON OFFICE:
108 Cannon House Office Building
Washington, DC 20515-3601
(202) 225-2211
Fax: (202) 225-9187

DISTRICT OFFICE:
2424 E. 21st Street, Suite 510
Tulsa, OK 74114-1741
(918) 749-0014
Fax: (918) 749-0781

Congress of the United States
House of Representatives
Washington, DC 20515-3601

COMMITTEE ON COMMERCE

SUBCOMMITTEES:
ENERGY AND POWER
TELECOMMUNICATIONS, TRADE, AND CONSUMER PROTECTION
FINANCE AND HAZARDOUS MATERIALS

March 20, 2001

The Honorable George W. Bush
President of the United States
The White House
1600 Pennsylvania Avenue
Washington, D.C. 20500

Dear Mr. President:

I am writing to you with the hope that you will consider honoring the 1951 University of San Francisco Dons football team at the White House. Some college football history may be helpful. The 1951 USF Dons were unbeaten, untied, and unfortunately largely unrecognized despite the fact that the USF team was arguably the best team of the 1951 season.

The Dons had been invited to play in the 1951 Orange Bowl with the pre-condition that the team's two African-American players would not play. The Dons who were, and continue to be a close knit team, adamantly refused the offer. You may be wondering who those two players are. One of the players is Ollie Matson, who went on to win two medals in the 1952 Helsinki Olympic Games followed by a successful 14 year career in the NFL. Upon his retirement he was inducted into the NFL Hall of Fame. The other player is Burl Toler who subsequently became the first black secondary school principal in San Francisco's history. And in another respect, Mr. Toler had the longest NFL career of any of his teammates, since he spent 25 years as a highly respected NFL referee.

On a personal note, Bob St. Clair, a member of the 1951 team, as well as a member of the NFL Hall of Fame, is a close friend of mine.

Because of your commitment to improved race relations, I am prevailing upon you to celebrate the 50th anniversary of the USF Dons unbeaten season. I know that the team members would certainly be honored and thrilled to commemorate the 1951 season with you at a White House ceremony, and I'm sure you would thoroughly enjoy meeting these fine men as well.

Whatever I can do to facilitate this request, please let me know. Thank you for your consideration.

Sincerely,

Steve Largent
Member of Congress

SML:rcb

Letter to President from Congressman Steve Largent

12
CHAPTER TWELVE
The Final Whistle

"It ain't over till it's over."

—Catcher Yogi Berra
New York Yankees

1952 Chicago Cardinals football card—
Head Coach Joe Kuharich

San Francisco Chronicle

The City's Only Home-Owned Newspaper

SATURDAY, JANUARY 31, 1981

Kuharich Lost His Battle,
But Won the War

By: Dave Anderson,
    New York Times (excerpt)

New York

Kuharich was an All American guard at Notre Dame and returned there in 1958 as head coach. His most successful season as a coach, however, occurred in 1951 when his University of San Francisco team was unbeaten in nine games. Nine players from that team went on to the NFL, including running back Ollie Matson, lineman Gino Marchetti, quarterback Ed Brown, tackles Bob St. Clair and Mike Mergen, guard Lou Stephens, defensive back Joe Scudero, and ends Ralph Thomas and Merrill Peacock. Marchetti and Matson are now in the Pro Football Hall of Fame.

The sports information director at USF that unbeaten season was Pete Rozelle, who delivered the eulogy at Kuharich's funeral this week.

Joe Kuharich died on Sunday, January 25, 1981—the day of Super Bowl XV.

*   *   *

San Francisco Chronicle

The City's Only Home-Owned Newspaper

OVERHEARD

USF GRIDDERS HAD EVERYTHING, BUT—

By Art Rosenbaum - sports columnist

USF began football in 1892 when it was known as St. Ignatius College. Tim Fitzpatrick (later to be known as Superior Judge Timothy I. Fitzpatrick) was the captain and the team played two games, losing one and tying one.

Since 1892, the Ignatians (later to be styled the Dons) sought the one perfect, unbeaten season. Finally it arrived, in 1951. The Dons won 'em all. For the first time, too, a USF player, Ollie Matson, was named All American.

Had these players been wrapped in the uniform of USC or Ohio State or Oklahoma, they would have been celebrated in song and story forevermore. But the timing was bad. USF was on the financial football rocks. It was said that the string of victories had no place on the major scene, because USF didn't play many major teams.

But the years have proved that the unbeaten, uninvited and eventually disbanded 1951 USF team must rate among the greats.

And so the 1951ers of USF remain the anomaly of football. They had everything it took, except elusive fame.

*   *   *

Lorrie Laurence—1991

Lorrie Laurence—1951

Lorrie Aguirre Laurence has joined Art Rosenbaum for the final chapter of this book.

Lorrie was raised in the Eureka Valley district of San Francisco, she attended St. Paul's High School, City College of San Francisco and San Francisco State College.

In 1951 she was "going steady" with a USF senior/varsity football star and working at the S. F. Call-Bulletin. Her newspaper career continued with the San Francisco Chronicle and the Hearst Examiner. Taking early retirement in 1994, Lorrie works on assignment as a freelance writer and researcher. She is currently co-authoring a novel.

The Pen Is Mightier…

By: Lorrie Aguirre-Laurence

In 1951, San Francisco boasted of four major daily newspapers: the Thieriot Family's Chronicle (AM); Hearst's Examiner (AM) and Call-Bulletin (PM); and Scripps-Howard's Daily News (PM).

Every sports staffer covering the Dons narrated their season with both precise accounts of the games and numerous human interest stories. No team ever had such devoted 'cheerleaders' – sparking a rooting section that soon encompassed the city. We gloried in their victories (and knew they were unstoppable), we enjoyed the articles that spotlighted the players themselves (a charismatic bunch) and we, too, were devastated to read the headlines that shouted *No Bowl Bids* and *USF Quits Football* (*outrage with bowl execs and sadness for the Hilltoppers*).

The ensuing years brought scattered stories in mostly eastern papers about ex Dons now playing in the pros. But in 1991, a highly publicized fortieth reunion was to be celebrated in grand style.

This sparked a flurry of local and national newspaper and magazine articles, as well as videos aired by the NFL, ESPN, Fox Sports and ABC (SF) which rekindled interest in the long-forgotten saga of the undefeated, untied and uninvited. And by the time of their golden anniversary gala, a book was being written.

Embraced once again by the media, that 'elusive fame' is finally theirs, their story to be told and retold…such is the way legends are made.

The legend of the '51 University of the San Francisco Dons…'Dream Team' has begun.

REFERENCES

Chapter 1

Two Cousins College Football Emporium
www.2cuz.com/featires1951/html
1951 – 50 Years Ago
Ronnie Fuchs
January 2001

Chapter 2

San Francisco Chronicle
New York Times (excerpt)
Dave Anderson, columnist
January 31, 1981

San Francisco Chronicle
New York Times (excerpt)
Dave Anderson, columnist
quote by Morris Siegel, sportswriter - Washington Star
January 31, 1981

The Evening Bulletin
Pro Grid Head Incensed Over McKeever's Actions (excerpt)
Author unknown
February 13, 1948

The Evening Bulletin
The Character Builder
Cartoon of Coach Ed McKeever
By Lanning
February 13, 1948

Chapter 3

San Francisco Chronicle
Don Gridders Have Found a Liking for Straw Hats and Large Corning Olives
Will Connolly, sportswriter
September 3, 1950

Chapter 4

San Francisco Chronicle
A Wild Bunch: Party Times on the Hilltop
Bruce Jenkins, Chronicle sportswriter
December 30, 1977

Chapter 5

1951 USF Football Media Guide
USF Prospectus – 1951
Pete Rozelle, Athletic News Director,
University of San Francisco

San Francisco Foghorn
Kuharich Slates Team Scrimmage After 1ˢᵗ Week of Spring Drills
Al Schlarmann, USF Sports Editor
April 6, 1951

San Francisco Examiner
Sports Parade
Curley Grieve, Sports Editor
September 15, 1951

The Call-Bulletin
Dink Slaps PCC For Giving USF Runaround
Sked 'Freeze-Out' Back in Force
Dink Templeton, Call-Bulletin Special Writer
September 17, 1951

The Call-Bulletin
Daley Says: USF Team Best In History
Walt Daley, sportswriter
September 17, 1951

Chapter 6

San Francisco Examiner
USF Choice Over San Jose Tonight
Matson, Brown & Co. Flash Under Lights at Kezar
Curley Grieve, Examiner Sports Editor
September 21, 1951

San Francisco Examiner
Quote
Bucky Walters, sportswriter
October 20, 1951

New York Herald Tribune
Quote
Harold Rosenthal, sportswriter
October 21, 1951

Associated Press
Ollie One Of Best—Kuharich
Will Grimsley, sportswriter
October 23, 1951

San Francisco Chronicle
College of Pacific – Pre Game
Unbeaten Dons Face Pacific
Dick Friendlich, sportswriter
November 17, 1951

Stockton Record
Quote
John Peri
November 1951

Warner Bros.
The Replacements
Quote by Gene Hackman (paraphrased)
2000

Chapter 7

San Francisco Foghorn
SEVENTEEN SENIORS GAVE USF ITS FINEST FOOTBALL TEAM
Time Runs Out On Matson, Men Who Blocked For Him
Walt Johnson, Editor-in-Chief
November 30, 1951

Chapter 8

San Francisco Chronicle
POST SEASON
THE ORANGE Mayor Gets In Plug For USF
Author unknown
November1951

Pro!
Packers Edition
Packers Vs. St. Louis Cardinals
Lambeau Field
Yes, They Were Collegiate – 1951 USF Dons (excerpt)
Wells Twombly, columnist
November 11, 1973

San Francisco Foghorn
Bowl Excuse Is Weak
Al Schlarmann, USF Sports Editor
November 30, 1951

Sports Illustrated
Best Team You Never Heard Of (excerpt)
The '51 Dons were unbeaten – and unsung
Ron Fimrite
September 12, 1998

San Francisco Chronicle
USF, Loyola Quit Game Simultaneously
Kerr Still Has Job; 'Concerned Over Kids'
Bill Anderson, sportswriter
December 31, 1951

San Francisco Examiner
Kuharich: "Tragedy"
No Other Choice, Ex-Coach Says
Dick Toner
December 31, 1951

San Francisco Examiner
Tulsa Lands St. Clair; Don Backs 'Unheeded'
Bill Mulligan, Copy Editor – Sports
No Date

The Call-Bulletin
Joe's Thoughts With His Great 1951 Team As He Departs Hilltop
Jack McDonald, Sports Editor
No date

Chapter 9

San Francisco Chronicle
Glimpse into Grid Past : Dons Stocked the Pros
Darrell Wilson, sportswriter
March 6, 1968

Source unknown
The 1951 Dons: An NFL Bonanza
Author unknown
December 30, 1977

Pro Football Weekly
Pro Football History: The 1951 Dons
University of San Francisco was unusual football factory
Jim Campbell
July 26, 1999

Chapter 10

San Francisco Examiner
SPORTS FINAL EDITION
Dream Team
'51 Dons, reassembling this weekend,
may have been best in college football history
Dwight Chapin, Examiner Senior Writer
May 26, 1991

The Times-Picayune
New Orleans, Louisiana
51 Dons Deserved Better Fate
Peter Finney, columnist
January 29, 1994

The New York Times
Once Uninvited, Undefeated and
Unsung ,but No Longer Unappreciated
Dave Anderson
September 23, 2001

Chapter 11

San Francisco Chronicle
Giving '51 Dons Their Due
Presidential apology asked to atone for racist snub that kept greatest
USF football team from bowl games
Ken Garcia, columnist
July 8, 2000

Marin Independent Journal
Overdue honor for '51 Dons
Novato Woman works to get USF champs in White House
Dave Albee, I.J. reporter
April 10, 2001

Chapter 12

San Francisco Chronicle
Kuharich Lost His Battle, But Won the War (New York Times excerpt)
Dave Anderson
January 31, 1989

San Francisco Chronicle
OVERHEARD (excerpt)
USF Gridders had everything, but—
Art Rosenbaum, sports columnist
No date

The Pen Is Mightier…
Lorrie Aguirre Laurence
February 2002